A PREFACE TO

METAPHYSICS

SEVEN LECTURES

ON BEING

BY

JACQUES MARITAIN

AYER COMPANY PUBLISHERS, INC.
SALEM, NEW HAMPSHIRE 03079

Reprint Edition, 1987
AYER Company, Publishers, Inc.

Reprinted from a copy in
The Library, University of Illinois
at Urbana-Champaign

Manufactured in the United States of America

ISBN   0-8369-5807-1   73-2507

A
Preface
to
Metaphysics

SEVEN LECTURES ON
BEING

by

JACQUES MARITAIN

A MENTOR OMEGA BOOK
Published by the New American Library

BD
312
.M32
1987
15-9429
may 1993

Published as a MENTOR OMEGA BOOK
By Arrangement with Sheed & Ward, Inc.

FIRST PRINTING, MARCH, 1962

MENTOR TRADEMARK REG. U.S. PAT. OFF. AND FOREIGN COUNTRIES
REGISTERED TRADEMARK—MARCA REGISTRADA
HECHO EN CHICAGO, U.S.A.

MENTOR OMEGA BOOKS are published by
The New American Library of World Literature, Inc.
501 Madison Avenue, New York 22, New York

PRINTED IN THE UNITED STATES OF AMERICA

CONTENTS

A PREFACE TO
METAPHYSICS

FIRST LECTURE

INTRODUCTORY

I. Living Thomism

1. Thomism is not a museum piece. No doubt, like other systems of medieval philosophy, indeed, philosophic systems of all ages, it must be studied historically. All the great philosophies whether of the Middle Ages or any other period have that in their substance which to an extent triumphs over time. But Thomism does so more completely than any other since it harmonizes and exceeds them all, in a synthesis which transcends all its components. It is relevant to every epoch. It answers modern problems, both theoretical and practical. In face of contemporary aspirations and perplexities, it displays a power to fashion and emancipate the mind. We therefore look to Thomism at the present day to save: in the speculative order, intellectual values; in the practical order, so far as they can be saved by philosophy, human values.

In short, we are concerned not with an archaeological

9

but with a living Thomism. It is our duty to grasp the reality and the requirements of such a philosophy.

This duty gives rise to a double obligation. We must defend the traditional wisdom and the continuity of the *Philosophia Perennis* against the prejudices of modern individualism, insofar as it values, seeks, and delights in novelty for its own sake, and is interested in a system of thought only insofar as it is a creation, the creation of a novel conception of the world. But equally we must show that this wisdom is eternally young and always inventive, and involves a fundamental need, inherent in its very being, to grow and renew itself. And so doing we must combat the prejudices of those who would fix it at a particular stage of its development and fail to understand its essentially progressive nature.

II. Metaphysics Are of Necessity Traditional and Permanent

2. We must recall the Thomist view of human teaching. We must remember that man is a social animal primarily because he is in need of teaching, and the teacher's art, like the doctor's, co-operates with nature, so that the *principal agent* in the art of instruction is not the teacher imparting knowledge to his pupil and producing it in his mind, but the understanding, the intellectual vitality of the pupil who receives that is to say, assimilates, the knowledge actively into his mind and so brings knowledge to birth there. But we must not forget that without the transmission of ideas elaborated by successive generations the individual mind could make little progress in the research and discovery of truth. In view of this fact the need of a tradition is evident. Obviously, to reject the continuity produced by the common labor of generations and the transmission of a doctrinal deposit—above all in the very order of understanding and knowledge—is to opt

for darkness. But do not the facts give the lie to my thesis, however obvious it may seem? Revolutions of technique and in the natural sciences present us with the spectacle of progress by *substitution,* and this, moreover, as a general and seemingly universal phenomenon. The railway has replaced the stagecoach, electric light the oil lamp. Einstein's system has dethroned Newton's, as the Copernican had dethroned the Ptolemaic astronomy. We are strongly tempted to generalize, to believe that this type of progress should be extended to every domain of intellectual activity. Was not medieval philosophy replaced by the Cartesian? Did not Kant oust Descartes, to be ousted in turn by Bergson, and will not Bergson make way for some other philosopher, Whitehead, perhaps, or Heidegger? And while we still wait for the advent of an antideterminist variety of materialism, a revival of hylozoism is taking shape under the dictatorship of the proletariat.

In view of all this we are shocked if we are told of a knowledge which applies today the same fundamental concepts, the same principles, as in the days of San-Lhara, Aristotle, or St. Thomas.

3. I have often answered this objection by pointing out that it is a gross blunder to confuse the art of the philosopher with the art of the tailor or milliner. I have shown also that truth cannot be subjected to a chronological test. Nevertheless the question must be examined more thoroughly. We shall then distinguish two very different types of progress, proper, respectively, to wisdom and the science of phenomena.

"Mystery" and "Problem"

4. Making use of terminology borrowed from a contemporary French philosopher, M. Gabriel Marcel,[1] though I am employing it in a completely different sense, we may say that every scientific question presents a double aspect, the one a *Mystery*, the other a *Problem*. It is a mystery and at the same time a problem, a mystery in regard to the thing, the object as it exists outside the mind, a problem in regard to our formulae.

An intelligible mystery is not a contradiction in terms. On the contrary, it is the most exact description of reality. Mystery is not the implacable adversary of understanding. This unreal opposition was introduced by Descartes and his Cartesian reason, though it is indeed inevitable in an idealist system or an idealist atmosphere. The objectivity of the understanding is itself supremely mysterious and the object of knowledge is "Mystery" reduced to a state of intelligibility in act and of intellection in act. In the act of understanding, the intellect becomes what is other than itself, precisely as such. It introduces into itself an inexhaustible (transobjective) [2] reality vitally apprehended as its object. Its object is reality itself. Like the act of faith the act of understanding does not stop at the formula but attains the object, *non terminetur ad enuntiabile, sed ad rem.*[3] The "Mystery" is its food, the *other* which it assimilates.

The proper object of understanding is being. And being is a mystery, either because it is too pregnant with

[1] See Gabriel Marcel, *Position et Approches du mystère ontologique* (Le Monde Cassé, Paris, Desclée de Brouwer, 1933).

[2] On this term see my *Les Degrés du Savoir*, Ch. III, p. 176 sqq.

[3] Sum Theol. II–II, i, 2 ad 2.

intelligibility, too pure for our intellect, which is the case with spiritual things, or because its nature presents a more or less impenetrable barrier to understanding, a barrier due to the element of nonbeing in it, which is the case with becoming, potency and, above all, matter.

The mystery we conclude is a fullness of being with which the intellect enters into a vital union and into ' which it plunges without exhausting it. Could it do so it would be God, *ipsum Esse subsistens* and the author of being. The Supreme "Mystery" is the supernatural Mystery which is the object of faith and theology. It is concerned with the Godhead Itself, the interior life of God, to which our intellect cannot rise by its unaided natural powers. But philosophy and science also are concerned with mystery, another mystery, the mystery of nature and the mystery of being. A philosophy unaware of mystery would not be a philosophy.

Where then shall we discover the pure type of what I call the "problem"? In a crossword puzzle, or an anagram.

At this extreme there is *no* ontological content. There is an intellectual difficulty with no being behind it. There is a logical difficulty, a tangle of concepts, twisted by a mind which another mind seeks to unravel. When the tangle has been unraveled, the difficulty solved, there is nothing further, nothing more to be known. For the only thing to be discovered was how to disentangle the threads. When Oedipus has discovered the key to the riddle, he can proceed on his way leaving the Sphinx behind him. The "problem" may be described as a notional complex created by our intellect, which at first appears inextricable and which must be disentangled. I am speaking of the problem in its pure state. You will soon see that there are other cases in which the "problem" aspect reappears, but no longer isolated, in combination with the "mystery" aspect.

5. In fact every cognitive act, every form of knowledge presents these two aspects. The mystery and the problem are *combined*. The mystery is present because

there is always some degree of being, and its depth and thickness must be penetrated. The problem also because our nature is such that we can penetrate being only by our conceptual formulae, and the latter of their nature compose a problem to be solved.

But according to the particular kind of knowledge one or the other aspect is predominant.

The problem aspect naturally predominates where knowledge is least ontological, for example, when it is primarily concerned with mental constructions built up around a sensible datum—as in empirical knowledge, and in the sciences of phenomena; or again when its objects are entities constituted or reconstituted by the intellect, which though certainly based on reality, need not exist outside the mind but may equally well be purely ideal as in mathematics; or yet again when its object is mental constructions of the practical intellect as in craftsmanship and applied science. It is, in fact, in this third category that the problem aspect is particularly evident. In mathematics and the sciences of phenomena it is well to the fore and indeed predominates. But the mystery aspect is also very pronounced, especially when a discovery is made or when a science is revolutionized or passes through a crisis.

The mystery aspect, as we should expect, predominates where knowledge is most ontological, where it seeks to discover, either intuitively or by analogy, being in itself and the secrets of being; the secrets of being, of knowledge and of love, of purely spiritual realities, of the First Cause (above all of God's interior life). The mystery aspect is predominant in the philosophy of nature and still more in metaphysics. And, most of all, in theology.

Where the problem aspect prevails one solution follows another: where one ends, the other begins. There is a rectilinear progress of successive mental views or ideal perspectives, of different ways of conceptualizing the object. And if one solution is incomplete, as is always the case, it is *replaced* by its successor. It is as when the landscape changes and scene succeeds to scene as the traveler proceeds on his way. Similarly the mind is on the move. Progress of this kind is progress by substitution.

On the other hand, where the mystery aspect prevails the intellect has to penetrate more and more deeply the *same* object. The mind is stationary turning around a fixed point. Or rather it pierces further and further into the same depth. This is progress in the same place, progress by *deepening*. Thus the intellect, as its habitus grows more intense, continues, as John of Saint Thomas puts it, to assault its object, the same object, with increasing force and penetration, *vehementius et profundius*. Thus we can read and reread the same book, the Bible, for example, and every time discover something new and more profound. Obviously, under the conditions of human life, progress of this kind requires an intellectual tradition, the firm continuity of a system based on principles which do not change.

Here knowledge is not exactly constituted by the addition of parts, still less by the substitution of one part for another. It is the whole itself that grows or rather is more deeply penetrated (every spatial metaphor is inadequate) as an indivisible whole and in all its parts at once.

6. At this point we must distinguish three kinds of intellectual thirst and three corresponding means of quenching them.

In the first case, where the problem aspect predominates, I thirst to know the answer to my problem. And when I have obtained the answer I am satisfied: *that particular* thirst is quenched. But I thirst for something else. And so interminably.

This is the water of science, useful and bitter.

In the second case, where the mystery aspect predominates, I thirst to know reality, *being* under one or other of its modes, the ontological mystery. When I know it I drink my fill. But I still thirst and continue to thirst for the same thing, the same reality which at once satisfies and increases my desire. Thus I never cease quenching my thirst from the same spring of water which is ever fresh and yet I always thirst for it.

This is the water of created wisdom.

To this wisdom the text may be applied, "They who eat me hunger still and they who drink me still thirst." [4]

In the third case—the vision of God's Word face to face—my thirst is again different. I thirst to see God and when I see Him my thirst will be completely quenched. I shall thirst no longer. And this is already in a measure true of the earthly commencement of bliss, the participation in time of eternal life.

This is the water of uncreated wisdom of which it is written "Whosoever drinketh of the water that I shall give him shall never thirst, but the water that I shall give him shall become in him a fountain of water springing up unto everlasting life." [5]

The climax of spiritual disorder is to confuse the third of these thirsts with the first, by treating the things of eternal life, the vision of God, as an object of the first thirst, that namely which belongs to the first case of which I was just speaking, the category of knowledge in which the *problem* predominates. For this is to treat beatitude, not as a mystery, our mystery par excellence, but as a problem or series of problems, like the solution of a puzzle. As a result of this confusion Leibnitz can declare that beatitude is a moving from one pleasure to another, and Lessing that he prefers endless research to the possession of truth which would be *monotonous*, and Kant considers the boredom which it would seem God must experience in the everlasting contemplation of Himself.

But it is also a radical disorder to confuse the second thirst with the first by treating philosophy, metaphysics, wisdom—a category of knowledge in which *reverence* for the mystery of being is the highest factor—as an object of the first thirst, pre-eminently a problem to answer, a puzzle to solve. Those who make this mistake attempt to

[4] Ecclesiasticus xxxiv. 20.
[5] John iv. 13–14.

make progress in wisdom by proceeding from puzzle to
puzzle, replacing one problem by another, one *Weltan-
schauung* by its successor, as though in virtue of an ir-
refragable law. Progress by substitution is required by
the sciences of phenomena, is their law, and the more
perfectly they realize their type the more progress they
make. But progress of this kind is not the law of wisdom.
Its progress is progress by an adhesion of the mind to
its object and a union with it increasingly profound, progress as it were by a growing intimacy. And it therefore
requires as its indispensable prerequisite a stable body of
doctrine and a continuous intellectual tradition.

7. Two considerations may now be advanced which
reinforce the proof that a philosophic tradition and a
stable continuity are indispensable for wisdom.

The first of these is provided by Christian thought and
its force is therefore confined to Christians. It concerns
the relation between philosophy and theology.

Since it is founded on the words of God, indeed upon
the *Word* of God, it is obvious that theology must be
permanent. "Heaven and earth shall pass away, but my
words shall not pass away." The science, rooted in the
faith, which develops and explains in terms of conceptual
reasoning the meaning of these divine words—the science
we call theology—cannot therefore be substantially
changed in the course of time, cannot progress by successive substitutions. It does progress, but of all sciences
built up by discursive reasoning, its progress is the most
stable and, more perfectly than the progress of any other
science, is a progress by entering ever more intimately.

Theology, however, makes use of philosophy. Philosophy is the means and the instrument of its development.
Philosophy, therefore, must be in its own fashion also
permanent.

That is why the Christian, we may remark, finds the
notion of a permanent philosophic wisdom easier to accept. For superior to philosophy but connected with it he
possesses a typical example of a science rooted in
mystery.

There is, however, a certain risk that we may confuse these two kinds of certainty and stability, those proper respectively to theology and philosophy, and ascribe to philosophy and its doctrinal continuity the stability of a higher order peculiar to theology. It is true that even the stability of theology is not absolute, for its continuity is not immutability but progress by penetration and admits, therefore, of many discoveries, renewals, and unexpected explanations. But even so theology is far more strictly and essentially traditional than philosophy. Its continuity is of another order and imitates more closely the immutability of Uncreated Wisdom.

8. The second confirmation is the spectacle of modern man and the modern mind. It thus possesses special weight for us moderns. I have in mind what may be called the peculiar experience of the modern world, all the attempts it has made to alter the nature of wisdom. The experiment has certainly been carried out. After Descartes had denied the scientific value of theology, and Kant the scientific value of metaphysics, we have witnessed human reason gone astray and a captive to empiricism seeking wisdom more anxiously than ever before, yet failing to find it, because it has rejected the sense of mystery and has attempted to subject wisdom to the alien law of progress by substitution. It turns now toward the east, now toward the west. Will wisdom come from one quarter or the other? It does not even possess the criteria by which wisdom could be recognized and is blown about by every chance wind of desire.

It is a remarkable fact that Thomas Aquinas did not impress the form of his wisdom on the final phase of medieval culture. From this point of view Thomism was not "a cultural success" on medieval soil.

It has been, so to speak, laid up in the heaven of the Church. St. Thomas thus belongs to the Church's great gift of prophecy. He assumes the figure, if I may so put it, of a prophetic saint, a prophetic sage. He is a saint reserved for the future. His reappearance in our time, as leader of a universal movement of philosophic inquiry, the advent of a period in the development of Thomism unlike any that went before it, assumes when viewed in this light a most striking significance. In the depths of the mind we hear the summons to fashion a universal Christian wisdom at the very moment when the progress of the sciences and of reflection enable us to give it its full scope and when the world, everywhere laboring under the same distresses and increasingly united in its culture and the problems with which it is faced, can or *could* be molded into conformity with this wisdom. May we say that it *still could be* molded or must we say that it *could have been* molded if only the clerks, as M. Benda calls them, had but understood and willed accordingly, fashioned by this wisdom to receive from it a reasonable order?

III. *Metaphysics is Necessarily Progressive and Inventive*

9. I have spoken of the obligation imposed upon us by the continuity of wisdom. I have now to speak of another also of urgent necessity. We have not only to defend the value and necessity of a philosophic tradition against the prejudices of minds revolutionary on principle. We must also take due account of the constant novelty characteristic of philosophic wisdom, and defend the necessity of renovation and growth inherent in its nature, in this case against the prejudices of minds conservative on principle and hidebound.

As we know, it was the task of St. Thomas to renovate the older scholasticism. It is a similar task which Thomists are called upon to perform today, a task whose novelty may well be greater than they themselves realize. In this connection many questions require examination and a complete analysis needs to be undertaken. For this there is no time. It must suffice to point out the fact.

But if you have understood what has just been explained you will understand that this work must be ac-

complished without detriment to the fixity of principles.
Nor must it be accomplished by adding heterogeneous
parts after the fashion in which those branches of knowledge progress in which the problem aspect, the puzzle,
tends to become as important as the mystery aspect. For
this reason I dislike the term "Neo-scholasticism" or
"Neo-Thomism." It involves the risk of pulling us down
from the higher plane of wisdom to the lower plane of
the problematic sciences and thereby leading us logically
to demand for Thomism also a progress by substitution in
which the *Neo* would devour the Thomism.

This work must be accomplished by a vital assimila-
tion and an immanent progress—as it were, by the progressive autogenesis of the *same* intellectual organism,
constantly building up and entering into *itself*, by a species
of transfiguration of which the growth of corporeal organisms is a very imperfect image. Think of a baby and
that baby grown to an adult. Its metaphysical personality
has not changed, it remains entire. Nor have any heterogeneous parts been engrafted from without. But everything in that human individual has been transfigured, has
become more differentiated, stronger, better proportioned.
At every decisive phase of growth the man has been more
profoundly transfigured while remaining more profoundly
himself and realizing himself more perfectly.

10. The part played in a progress of this kind by other
philosophic systems is considerable. As I have pointed
out elsewhere,[6] a system with faulty foundations is a
system adapted to the vision of one epoch and one epoch
alone. For this very reason its less solid armor enables it
to throw itself more quickly—though only to perish—
upon the novel aspects of truth appearing above the contemporary horizon. All these systems which lack a sufficient foundation compose a merely potential philosophy, a
philosophy in a state of flux, covering contradictory formulas and irreconcilable doctrines and upheld by whatever truth these may contain.

[6] *Les Degrés du Savoir*, Preface.

If there exists on earth a philosophic system securely based on true principles, and such I believe Thomism to be, it will incorporate—with more or less delay due to the intellectual laziness of Thomists—and thus progressively *realize* in itself this potential philosophy which will thereby become to that extent visible and capable of formulation, formed and organically articulated. Thus, in my opinion, Thomism is destined to bear with it, in its own progress, the progress of philosophy. By assimilating whatever truth is contained in these partial systems it will expand its own substance and deduce from it more and more penetrating shafts of light, which will reveal the forces concealed in its truths. The novelty which it thus displays, though not seeking it for its own sake, is above all a novel approach to the same shores of being, a new distribution of the same wealth, the pregnant mystery of things. New prospects are being constantly opened up of the same intelligible world, the same incorporeal landscape, which seem to transform it before our eyes and make us enter more deeply into the secrets of its beauty.

11. A particular question must be raised at this point, that of vocabulary. The fundamental concepts remain the same, they do not *change*. But we must reach them by new paths, so far at least as the method of treatment is concerned. The question arises whether the old names are still appropriate in all cases.

In this connection we must bear in mind that the fashion in which the ancients formed their philosophical vocabulary was admirably spontaneous, supple, and living, but also imperfect and almost excessively natural. They relied with a robust confidence upon common sense and upon the language which objects utter by their sensible appearances. For their intuitive intelligence was sufficiently powerful and sufficiently fresh to transcend these media. Thus it was that when they defined living being they thought primarily of that which changes its position, moves of itself. There is, in fact, no better definition. But it requires a prolonged critical examination and elaboration. The terminology of the ancients was apparently—I

mean in respect of the objects from which the metaphorical signification was derived—more material than
our own, not at all to the taste of our more refined con-
temporaries. In reality—that is, in respect of the meaning itself—it was more spiritual and went straight to the
heart of things.

Because today we have become duller ourselves and
more exacting, we require a vocabulary less charged with
matter, less spontaneous, more remote from the senses,
or rather renovated by a new contact—more penetrating
and more deliberate, like our art itself—with sensible objects, by a new germination of the mental word in ourselves. In this respect philosophy is in the same case as
poetry. Like poetic images philosophic terms are blunted.
The creation of a new vocabulary by depriving the understanding of the assistance provided by custom and by a
social security already achieved compels it to pay exclusive attention to the vital process in which the idea is
born of images and phantasms and the experience of
life.

Though these questions of vocabulary are not unimportant, their importance is obviously secondary in comparison with doctrine. Nor must we forget that although
these innovations of terminology are calculated to di-
minish certain obstacles produced in many modern minds
by the influence, which is in truth below the level of
philosophy, of associated ideas and by the reactions of
sensibility, they will never make the voice of intelligible
being audible to those who lack the ear for it or who
close their ears to it. Nor will they suffice to create a
vocabulary common to all philosophers. For terminology
is essentially dependent upon doctrine, and a common
vocabulary presupposes a common doctrine.

> All life and joy is motion. That of time and vulgar
> souls is linear, and so not without change of place;
> and good to them is known only in the coming and
> going. With souls of grace it is not so. They go about
> a centre, which planetary motion is their joy. They
> have also a self-revolving motion which is their peace.

Their own regularity enables them to perceive the order of the universe. Their ears with inmost delectation catch the sound of the revolving spheres. They live in fruition of the eternal novelty.[7]

[7] Coventry Patmore, *Aphorisms and Extracts.*

SECOND LECTURE

COUNTERFEIT METAPHYSICAL COIN

I. The Object of These Three Lectures on Being

1. In this and the two following lessons I want to invite your particular attention to the subject matter of metaphysics, *being* as such. I shall not adopt any formal academic procedure, but shall rather attempt to bring home to you certain preliminary truths on which too little stress is often laid at the outset, though the mental attitude of modern philosophers educated in idealism makes it particularly necessary to do so.

The most important texts dealing with the questions treated in this lecture and the next are Aristotle's *Metaphysics* and St. Thomas' *Commentaries* (St. Thomas' *Præmium*, Book III [B], Lecture 12, and above all Book IV, Lectures 1 and 4; also Book VI, particularly the first two lectures). You may also consult the two works of Père Garrigou-Lagrange on the *Philosophy of Being* and on *God* and Cajetan's Commentary on the *De Ente et Essentia.*

24

Statement of the Problem

2. As you know, it is a fundamental doctrine of scholastic philosophy that the formal object of the intellect is being. In the case of the human intellect there are two levels, two states, or two quite distinct phases to be taken account of.

In the first place the Thomists, and in particular Cajetan, inquire what is the object first attained by the human intellect, an object therefore which every man attains the instant he begins to think as a rational being, an object presented from the outset to the human mind. They answer with Cajetan: it is being as enveloped or embodied in the sensible quiddity, being "clothed" in the diverse natures apprehended by the senses, *ens concretum quidditati sensibili.*

It is something confiscally contained in this or that particular nature, for example, in the dog, the horse, the pebble, something clothed in this or that object and diversified by it. It is not, therefore, the element common to all these things, disengaged from them, *extricated* in its purity. Nor yet is it diversity in its pure state, that is to say, the manifold of diverse essences and diverse sensible quiddities. It is at the same time the particular quiddity and being in general. It is being as enveloped, embodied, in the manifold of natures or essences. This is what the Thomists teach us of the object attained primarily and in the first instance by the human intellect. But we must be quite clear that this is not the object of metaphysics. If it were, a child, as soon as he begins to perceive objects intellectually, would already be a metaphysician. For the object of which we are speaking is the object which the intellect attains primarily and in the first instance.

The object of metaphysics—and we now pass to an altogether different level, an entirely different phase in the process of human intellection—is, according to the Thomists, being as such, *ens in quantum ens*, being not clothed or embodied in the sensible quiddity, the essence or nature of sensible things, but on the contrary *abstractum,* being disengaged and isolated, at least so far as being can be taken in abstraction from more particularized objects. It is being disengaged and isolated from the sensible quiddity, being viewed as such and set apart in its pure intelligible values.

Metaphysics, therefore, at the summit of natural knowledge, where it becomes fully wisdom, brings to light in its pure values and uncovers what is enveloped and veiled in the most primitive intellectual knowledge. You can see how dangerous it would be to confuse these two phases, these two states, and to imagine, as so many modern philosophers believe, that for the Thomist the metaphysical habitus is specified by being as it is primarily attained by our intellect.

3. Observe that being presents two aspects. One of these is its aspect as *essence* which corresponds particularly to the first operation of the mind. For we form concepts primarily in order to apprehend, though in many cases blindly, essences—which are positive capacities of existence. The other is the aspect existence, the *esse* in the strict sense, which is the end in which things attain their achievement, their act, their "energy" par excellence, the supreme actuality of whatever is. Nor must we suppose that this second aspect, this aspect which crowns and perfects being, escapes the grasp of the intellect. The Platonists show a general tendency to confine the object of the human intellect to essences, whereas the profound tendency of St. Thomas' philosophy leads the intellect, and therefore philosophy and metaphysics, not only to essences but to existence itself, the perfect and perfecting goal, the ultimate fulfillment of being.

It is in the second operation of the mind, in the judgment, by composition and division, that the speculative intellect grasps being, not only from the standpoint of essence but from that of existence itself, actual or possible. Existence is here apprehended *ut exercita,* that is as actualized by a subject; not merely as presented to the mind, as is the case with the simple concept of existence, but as possessed potentially or actually by a subject. Therefore Cajetan can say in a phrase full of meaning for the metaphysician that it is not contradictory to say *existentia non existit,* existence does not exist. For the term *existentia,* the concept and the term existence designates existence itself from the standpoint of essence, inasmuch as it is an intelligible concretion, a focus of intelligible determination, *existentia ut significata,* as apprehended by a concept. On the other hand, since existence when it is posited in the judgment and by the verb which expresses the judgment is attained *ut exercita,* as actualized or possessed, it would be an obvious contradiction to say, "What exists does not exist," *Quod existit non existit.* And it is the judgment that completes and perfects knowledge. It is a radical error to restrict the object of the intellect to the object of the first operation of the mind. Unfortunately a number of popular expositions of scholasticism seem to represent the matter in this false light. They speak as though the object of the first operation constitutes the object of intellection as such. This is quite untrue. It is merely a preparation for the second, which achieves knowledge.

When we affirm that the object of the intellect is being, an affirmation which displays the profound realism of Thomist philosophy, we do not stop short at essences. It is to existence itself that the intellect proceeds when it formulates within itself a judgment corresponding to what a thing is or is not outside the mind. From this point of view the intellect and the will are on the same footing, though there is also a fundamental difference between the two cases. The goal of the will is existence precisely as outside the mind, as actualized or *possessed* by reality external to the mind, outside the spiritual act of

the will. But the intellect and its act are fulfilled by
existence affirmed or denied by a judgment, by existence
attained—as it is lived or *possessed* by a subject—within
the mind, within the mind's intellectual act itself.

A Digression on Existence and Philosophy

4. If the distinctive object of the intellect is being, not
only "essential" or quidditative but existential, it is clear
that philosophy must be orientated to being in the same
way. It seeks existence itself, though not, as is the case
with practical philosophy, to produce it, but to know it.

Where actual existence is necessary and is thus able as
such to perfect a knowledge which is thus rendered complete—science in the strict sense—philosophy proceeds to
actual existence, something which actually exists. It is
natural theology and tends to the Cause of being, God,
Whose essence is His own eternally actual existence.

Philosophy, because it is science in the strictest sense
—*noblesse oblige*—must find its object in that which cannot be annulled, intelligible necessities. Therefore where
existence is contingent, simply posited as a fact, as is the
case with all created being, it must, because of this defect
in its object, be directly orientated only to possible existence. Which does not mean that it is restricted to a realm
of pure essences. Its goal is still existence. It considers
the essences as capable of actualization, of being posited
outside the mind. This is involved by the fact that the
judgment is the perfection of knowledge and of the act
of intelligence. And this means that philosophy considers
essences insofar as they require to issue forth and communicate themselves, to combine or separate in existence.
In short, it considers them from the standpoint of the
affluence and generosity of being. But this is not all. As
the intellect "in a way leaving its proper sphere betakes
itself by the instrumentality of the senses to corruptible

things in which the universal is realized," [1] so philosophy returns by the instrumentality of the senses to the actual existence of the object of thought which it contemplates.

The philosophy of nature which verifies its conclusions by sense date refers to the corruptible existence which alone can be attained by sensation in order to establish scientifically *what are* the objects it studies—not only to know their mode of existence but also to know their essence.

Metaphysics, however, does not verify its conclusions in sense data, nor, like mathematics, in the imagination. Nevertheless, it too refers to the corruptible existence which can be attained by sensation. But it does so not to establish scientifically what are the realities it studies—those namely which constitute the subject matter of metaphysics,[2] the being "common to the ten predicaments," created and material being taken as being —nor in order to know their essence. It does so to know how they exist, for this, too, metaphysics should know, to attain their mode of existence, and then to conceive by analogy the existence of that which exists immaterially, which is purely spiritual.

The part played by the senses is, you see, absolutely indispensable. Every judgment must in one way or another be finally resolved in them. In other words, the *res sensibilis visibilis*, the visible object of sense, is the touchstone of every judgment, *ex qua debemus de aliis judicare*, by which we must judge of everything else, because it is the touchstone of existence.[3] A metaphysician deprived of the senses or their use, a metaphysician asleep or dreaming, is for St. Thomas a sheer impossibility, a monster, an absurdity. And this not only because ideas are derived from the senses, but because the senses, which possess a speculative value, though it is obscure, are indispensable to science, and even to the

---

[1] Cajetan, *In Anal. Post,* I, I

[2] Cf. St. Thomas, *In Metaph. Præmium.*

[3] Cf. *De Veritate,* q. 12, a 12, ad. 3. *Les Degrés du Savoir,* p. 255.

supreme science, the science most disengaged from the material, if it is to reach the actual existence which it may neither ignore nor neglect. This is a corruptible existence which it attains only indirectly by leaving its proper sphere and through the instrumentality of the senses.

From this you will understand what kind of man the Thomist metaphysician should be. He should possess a sensitive body, be like St. Thomas himself *mollis carne.* Most certainly he must not be exclusively an intellect. His equipment of senses must be in good order. He must be keenly and profoundly aware of sensible objects. And he should be plunged into existence, steeped ever more deeply in it by a sensuous and aesthetic perception as acute as possible, and by experiencing the suffering and struggles of real life, so that aloft in the third heaven of natural understanding he may feed upon the intelligible substance of things. Is it necessary to add that the professor who is nothing but a professor, withdrawn from real life and *rendered insensible* at the third degree of abstraction, is the diametrical opposite of the genuine metaphysician? The Thomist philosopher is dubbed *scholastic,* a name derived from his most painful affliction. Scholastic pedantry is his peculiar foe. *He* must constantly triumph over his domestic adversary, the professor.

The Thomist philosophy, therefore, is, in the sense just explained, an *existential* philosophy. The phrase may be understood in many different ways. I have just shown you in what sense it is applicable to *the speculative philosophy* of Saint Thomas, Thomism in the very order of speculation, particularly metaphysical speculation.

In another sense the phrase is applicable to the *practical philosophy* of Saint Thomas. This tends to concrete acts which must be posited into existence. This time directly and in the distinctive sphere of its practicality —and not only indirectly, leaving its own sphere of action by means of the senses—the intellect, the practical intellect (*voluntate conjuncta*), tends to existence and lays hold of existence to regulate and determine it.

In a third sense which, however, pertains no longer to the domain of the intellect but to that of the will, thought may be termed *existential*, namely when it does not simply know the truth by yielding itself fully in accordance with the law of the mind to objective being, but when it, or rather the thinker, lives this truth, draws and assimilates it into his subjective being. It is in this third sense that many moderns, pre-eminently the Danish thinker, Sören Kierkegaard, understand the term existential. Too often they have made the tragic mistake of seeking the distinctive norm of philosophy, her law of knowledge, in the existential thus understood—which confuses everything.

Return To Our Problem

5. This digression was not superfluous. We shall now return to our theme. Being is the formal object of the intellect. Therefore whatever it knows and every time it knows it attains being. But what are we to say of the various sciences inferior to metaphysics? In these being is particularized. Such a science deals with being of a particular kind. The specific object of metaphysics, on the other hand, is being regarded in itself and in accordance with its distinctive mysteries, *ens secundum quod est ens*, as St. Thomas says, translating Aristotle (*Metaphysica*, Book V, Lecture I, 530–533 in the Cathala edition). There are weighty and authoritative texts here which it is most important to bear in mind.[4]

There is a science which studies being, investigates being

---

[4] *Met.* 5 (IV), I 1003, a, 21. "There is a science which investigates being as being, and the attributes which belong to it in virtue of its own nature. Now this is not the same as any of the so-called special sciences; for none of these deals generally with being as being. They cut off a part of being and investigate the attributes of this part—this is what the mathematical sciences for instance do. Now since we are seeking the first principles and the highest causes, clearly there must be something to which these belong in virtue of its own nature. If, then,

as such. This is its distinctive subject. And at the same time it studies the properties of being, the characteristics proper to being as such. The other sciences are concerned with particular kinds of being. Obviously they study being,

---

our predecessors who sought the elements of existing things were seeking these same principles, it is necessary that the elements must be elements of being not by accident but just because it is being. Therefore it is of being as being that we must also grasp the first causes." (Trans. W. D. Ross).

St. Thomas's Commentary on this passage (IV Lecture I, Ed. Cathala, 530–533):

"Dicit autem 'secundum quod est ens,' quia scientiae aliae, quae sunt de entibus particularibus, considerant quidem de ente, cum omnia subjecta scientiarum sint entia, non tamen considerant ens secundum quod ens, sed secundum quod est hujusmodi ens, scilicet vel numerus, vel linea, vel ignis, aut aliquid hujusmodi.

"Dicit etiam 'et quae huic insunt per se' et non simpliciter quae huic insunt, ad significandum quod ad scientiam non pertinet considerare de his quae per accidens insunt subjecto suo, sed solum de his quae per se insunt. Geometra enim non considerat de triangulo utrum sit cupreus vel ligneus, sed solum considerat ipsum absolute secundum quod habet tres angulos aequales, etc. Sic igitur hujusmodi scientia, cujus est ens subjectum, non oportet quod consideret de omnibus quae insunt enti per accidens, quia sic consideraret accidentia quaesita in omnibus scientiis, cum omnia accidentia insint alicui enti, non tamen secundum quod est ens. Quae enim sunt per se accidentia inferioris, per accidens se habent ad superius, sicut per se accidentia hominis non sunt per se accidentia animalia. Necessitas autem hujus scientiae quae speculatur ens et per se accidentia entis, ex hoc apparet, quia hujusmodi non debent ignota remanere, cum ex eis aliorum dependeat cognitio; sicut ex cognitione communium dependet cognitio rerum propriarum.

"Deinde cum dicit 'haec autem'. Hic ostendit, quod ista scientia non sit aliqua particularium scientiarum, (is not to be confused with any of the so-called special sciences) tali ratione. Nulla scientia particularis considerat ens universale inquantum hujusmodi, sed solum aliquam partem entis divisam ab aliis; circa quam speculatur per se accidens, sicut scientiae mathematicae aliquod ens speculantur, scilicet ens quantum. Scientia autem communis considerat universale ens secundum quod ens: ergo non est eadem alicui scientiarum particularium."

for all the subjects of the sciences are beings. But they do not study being as such, but insofar as it is being of a particular kind, number, for example, or geometrical figure or fire and so on.

You must read that first lecture of St. Thomas, which is devoted to establishing this point, because it is of the utmost importance if we are to grasp the Thomist conception of metaphysics. Metaphysics investigates the first 'principles of things and their highest causes. But these causes and principles are causes and principles of a particular kind of intelligible mystery, the intelligible mystery which is being itself. This science therefore investigates the principles of being as such. This, then, is the subject matter of metaphysics, which because it embraces all the rest beneath its sway and dominates them, is termed by Saint Thomas in the passage just quoted the "universal science," *scientia communis.*

The term, however, risks misinterpretation. We must beware of a fatal error, confusing metaphysics with logic. This mistake has, in fact, been made by the moderns, many of whom maintain that this being as such is a mere word, a linguistic residuum, or else that it is a universal frame whose value is purely logical, not ontological. According to them the metaphysician has fallen victim to human language, whereas in fact he passes through and beyond language to attain its intellectual source, superior to any uttered word. We must, therefore, understand clearly that the metaphysical intuition of being is *sui generis* and of powerful efficacy and therefore *distinguish carefully being which is the object of metaphysics from being as it is grasped by common sense and studied by the natural sciences and from being as studied by logic.* Failure to observe these distinctions has led many modern thinkers into very grave confusions. For when we speak to them of being as the object of metaphysics they assume, by a species of intellectual reflex, without even being conscious of the assumption, that we are speaking either of being as it is studied by logic or being as known by common sense, being as it is understood by all who employ the verb to be.

II

6. At this point further distinctions are necessary. When we consider the object first attained by the human intellect of which we were speaking above, namely being embodied in sensible natures, we find that it can be envisaged from two different points of view, either as it is apprehended by knowledge of sensible nature and the divers experimental sciences, or as it is apprehended by common sense.

Particularized Being

7. We shall consider first the natural sciences. As St. Thomas has just reminded us, though these sciences certainly study being, it is a being presented to the mind as differentiated, or masked, by particular conditions and a particular "behavior." Knowledge of nature considers sensible and mobile being either as the object of the *philosophy of nature*—which is intelligible being but considered with the particular qualification of mutability, that is, insofar as it is involved in the sensible and changing corporeal world—or as in the *empirical sciences*, being as the mere foundation of observable and measurable phenomena. We may designate as *particularized being* this being insofar as it is studied by the divers sciences of nature. The terminology I am suggesting is not the accepted terminology of the schools. It is simply a means of bringing home to you certain points of fundamental importance.

Now observe: for the sciences thus specified and demarcated not by *being* but by *being of a particular kind,* the notion of being taken as such has and can have no meaning. If we speak to a scientist of being as such, he can make nothing of it. For to the habitus which he represents it is nothing. By this I do not mean to say that the scientific-experimental habitus pronounces that it is nothing. For it would transgress its natural boundaries by pronouncing upon an object which is beyond its province. I say that the scientist as such can make no pronouncement on the subject. It is beyond his scope, and therefore he knows nothing of it.

Vague Being

8. If now we adopt the standpoint of common sense it is quite another matter. The perspective has entirely changed. For we are now confronted with an infra-scientific or pre-scientific knowledge, the term scientific being here understood in a universal sense as a perfect and certain knowledge, knowledge in the strict sense, knowledge by causes whether it is afforded by the divers particular sciences, by the philosophy of nature, or by metaphysical wisdom. The knowledge of common sense is a natural and spontaneous growth, the product, so to speak, of rational instincts, and has not yet attained the level of science. It is an infra-scientific knowledge. Nevertheless, this infra-scientific knowledge is more universal than that of the various particular sciences of which I have just spoken. It possesses a certain metaphysical value inasmuch as it attains the same objects as metaphysics attains in a different fashion. Common sense is therefore, as it were, a rough sketch of metaphysics, a vigorous and unreflective sketch drawn by the natural motion and spontaneous instincts of reason. This is why common sense attains a certain though unscientific knowledge of God, human personality, free will, and so on.

Here, indeed, is the being of the metaphysician. It has

a meaning for common sense. It is the hidden sinew of all that common sense knows of the things of the spirit. But it is not *known* as such. Otherwise every man would be a metaphysician, and the metaphysical habitus would not be, as it is, a sublime and exceedingly rare mental endowment. It would be simply common sense. In fact, being as such is apprehended blindly at this level, in a sign, an object of thought, which is, as it were, a *surrogate* and a *mask of being as such, ens in quantum ens.*

To be more precise: Speak to common sense of "being." Observe that common sense would not itself mention it. It reasons about particular objects basing itself implicitly on the being they possess. From the consideration of these particular objects it rises to their First Cause. And this ascent necessarily implies that means of proof which being is. For unless we consider the being in objects we could not rise to the First Cause of all being. But this operation of common sense is implicit, as is the support it finds in the object of thought, "being." By itself common sense cannot disengage this notion of being and envisage it in its distinctive mystery. Let the metaphysician, I say, talk to common sense and speak of "being as such." Common sense will not explicitly conceive this being of which he speaks otherwise than as the object of what Thomists call *abstractio totalis,* an abstraction which is pre-scientific and infra-scientific. (On this see Cajetan, Proemium to the *De Ente et Essentia,* and John of Saint Thomas, *Logic,* Secunda Pars, Q 27, Art. I.) What they term *abstractio totalis* we may call "extensive" abstraction.[5]

It is the mere disengagement of a universal from the many particulars it subsumes, the simple operation by which, before inquiring whether in what I call man there exists an original focus of intelligibility and what that focus is, I derive from *Peter* and *Paul* the object of thought "Man," then from *Man* in turn the object of thought "Animal," thus passing successively to increasing-

[5] The term proposed by M. Yves Simon *Introd. à l'Ontologie du Connaître,* p. 78.

ly general universals. The rich content of intelligible light remains implicit, as it were dormant. What appears explicitly is that on which the logical relations of greater or lesser generality are founded. This extensive abstraction is common to all knowledge, to pre-scientific knowledge as well as the scientific knowledge which presupposes the former. By hypothesis, on the level at which we are standing, we are envisaging objects from the point of view of common sense; consequently our knowledge of them is imperfect, not yet scientific. At this level no other hierarchy obtains between the concepts thus abstracted than that which arises from what the logician, as he reflects upon them, will term extensive relations. Thus, we perceive the notion of animal, for example, to be more extensive than that of man. But we have not yet explicitly disengaged what it is that distinguishes the former from the latter. For we are concerned with the confused and still imperfect notions of objects formed by common sense. Similarly we perceive the notion of being to be the most extensive, the widest of all notions. But we have not yet disengaged the properties of being as the primordial source and focus of intelligible mystery, and have not yet seen its distinctive countenance.

Observe that although what I am saying looks very simple, it is, in fact, very difficult: because we are trying to grasp what takes place in us at two different phases of knowledge which are expressed by the same words, indeed by the same word, being. We may live in the company of a man, yet not know the color of his eyes or the individual mystery of his soul. If we are asked who he is, we reply, my friend, the man who shares my amusements or my work. Yet we have not seen his unique psychological countenance.

It is the same with this object of thought, this primordial reality we call *being*. We have not looked it in the face. We think it something far simpler than it is. We have not yet troubled to unveil its true countenance. We do not suspect the peculiar mystery contained in the notion of it. For us, so far as our explicit knowledge is concerned, being is simply the most general and the most convenient of the classifications which we constantly employ and in which all the objects of our thought are arranged, the most comprehensive of them. It is merely a class.

This is true. But although common sense, when we mention being, explicitly thinks only of this most general class, nevertheless—and this second feature is as typical and as important as the first—it places in this class all the diverse objects of sense, all the varieties of being, a chaotic universe of innumerable forms, so that, if we may so put it, the comprehensive class *together with* the host of sensible objects which fill it is, as it were, the *practical equivalent and the surrogate* of the being which is the metaphysician's concern.

But it is not yet that being as the metaphysician is to see it and disengage it. Just now when I was speaking of the sciences inferior to metaphysics, I spoke of *particularized being*, masking and enveloping the metaphysical concept of being. In this case it is *vague being* that masks it. The metaphysical concept of being is present. But it is not disengaged but disguised, invisible. This vague being of common sense renders it possible to work upon what is really (though the user does not know it) the metaphysical notion of being, and thus reach true pre-philosophic conclusions about certain fundamental problems which the metaphysician will settle scientifically and philosophically. That is to say, we are here confronted with an imperfect state of knowledge and at the same time with a species of philosophy corresponding with it, which is not yet philosophy, not yet perfect knowledge, but the prefiguration and preliminary sketch of philosophy.

III

Being Divested of Reality

9. Hitherto we have been concerned with two ways in which being confronts the mind—or in which the term

being can designate a particular object of thought, namely *particularized being* as it is studied by the different sciences and *vague being* envisaged by common sense.

We have now to investigate what being is for the logician. It is no easy problem. As you know, the distinctive subject matter of logic according to St. Thomas is an *ens rationis*, a conceptual being, namely what is known, precisely as known. The objects which logic studies are not studied as they are in themselves but as they are involved in the process of reasoning, as they are within the mind as it moves toward truth. This is the conceptual being which is the special concern of logic. Logic deals with everything with which other branches of philosophy or the particular sciences deal, though it studies them not as they really are but as involved in the process of reasoning. The logician will therefore, as he proceeds, encounter the notion of being, as he encounters all the rest, and, moreover, more than other notions, since all other notions presuppose it. Being, we conclude, is studied by the logician under the formal aspect characteristic of his science, the formal aspect of a conceptual being of the logical variety, *sub ratione entis rationis logici*, that is to say, under the formal aspect of the conceptual order within the mind as it moves toward truth. Do not forget that logic is a reflex science in which the mind returns upon itself, upon the things it already knows, to study them and inquire how it has known them and in what order they are present within itself. Therefore being has already been apprehended by ordinary intelligence, and may equally well have been apprehended as such, *secundum quod ens,* by the metaphysician. But this intuition, this perception, is *presupposed* by the logician. It is not his business. It has already taken place. He turns back upon it to study it from his own reflex and logical point of view.

The logician returns reflexively to being as it plays a part in the order of thought proceeding toward truth, and in the vital relationships of concepts between themselves. For example, the notion of being is of the first importance in securing the coherence of thought, inasmuch as the whole of logic depends upon the principle of contradiction which is the logical form of the principle of identity: *non est negare et affirmare simul*. We cannot affirm and deny the same thing from the same point of view. The notion of being also plays a part in the theory of the verbal copula essential to the judgment. Finally, and this is a most important consideration, the logician studies from his reflex standpoint the transcendental and analogical character of being. He sees being as the most universal, the super-universal concept. He distinguishes reflexively and scientifically from the standpoint of his science the characteristic of maximal extension or supreme universality already discovered by vague being, that is, by being as the object of a simple *abstractio totalis*.

10. It is most important to understand that this being, which is studied by the logician and is bound up with the other distinctive objects of logic and involved in them all, is not the metaphysician's being. It presupposes the latter. But in logic being is apprehended as an object of secondary mental vision, *secunda intentio mentis*. Reflex knowledge of the mind's own intellectual process and of objects as they are present in the mind is the objective light of logic. That which gives logic its specific character, the formal aspect under which it studies objects, is conceptual being, which *cannot* exist outside the mind. *Being* itself is envisaged by logic under this formal aspect of conceptual being. The logician, therefore, studies being under an aspect in which it can exist only in the mind, an aspect in which it cannot really exist.

The logician's being differs in this from the metaphysician's in that it is envisaged as present in the mind and can exist in the mind alone. In short, all its real functions are presupposed but are not formally studied by the logician. What the logician formally disengages are the functions of being in and for knowledge which are functions of the conceptual order. Even if we have already looked being in the face, now in logic we behold it only as reflected in our eyes, as it has entered into the process of our reasoning and knowledge. The logician's being may thus be termed reflected being or *being divested of reality*.

It is immediately obvious that if the logician's being is mistaken for the object of a science of reality, this science will necessarily be a science of the void, of vacuity itself. For by definition none of the real functions of being, but only its conceptual functions, are the proper and the direct object of logical study. There could be no more serious error than to suppose that the being of metaphysics is this being envisaged under the aspect of conceptual being, the being which belongs to the distinctive subject matter of logic and is apprehended by the objective light distinctive of logic.

Pseudo-Being

11. At this point some further considerations arise. We must take note of a *decadence* which has occurred in the history of philosophy.

I shall point out here its principal stages.

Notice in the first place two errors concerned with logic itself. The first of these was to give extension precedence over comprehension (intension) until the latter was at last completely forgotten and account taken only of the former. If, however, we neglect the characters which intrinsically constitute an object of thought and consider solely its greater or lesser extension, there is no longer any reason to distinguish being, as the ancients distinguished it, from conceptual objects of a purely generic nature. Being becomes a genus, a class, the widest of all. It is termed a genus, the supreme genus. In the eyes of the scholastic philosopher this is a serious heresy. Being is most certainly not a genus but a transcendental. Notice what follows. How shall we proceed to reach this supreme genus? You may not introduce into the definition of the genus *animal* the characteristic notes of one of its species, *man* for example. To conceive animal you must make abstraction of whatever belongs to man alone. That is to say, to arrive at the genus you eliminate whatever is distinctive of the species. What, then, if being is simply a genus? To reach this supreme genus you will be obliged to eliminate all the varieties of being, all the determinations which particularize it. In short, to arrive at the genus being you will be compelled to eliminate *everything which is* and you will thus reach a being indistinguishable from nothing. This was Hegel's procedure. Because he had forgotten that being is a transcendental, he was logically compelled to identify being with nonentity.

The second error concerns the very nature of logic. Many moderns, particularly since Kant and Hamilton, call logic formal in a very different sense from that in which the ancients so termed it. For them it is a science of the laws and forms of a thought *divorced* from things and independent of them. In this conception of logic its object is no longer things themselves, though as transported into the mind, but pure forms of thought, as though knowledge had a structure and forms independent of things and the logician studied these forms and this structure of thought. Thus the bridge is broken between thought and things, and the logician's being no longer presupposes real being. It is a pure form of thought.

12. A third error, this time a metaphysical error, is to assign as the specific object of metaphysics essences as such, and not to require the intellect to proceed, as its nature craves, to existence, to *esse*, I mean *esse ut exercitum*, actual or possible, which, as I have shown above, implies that it returns through the instrumentality of the senses to the actual existence of corruptible things. Thus the bridge is broken between metaphysics and existence. Metaphysics stops short at the description of essences. If it envisages *esse* and is orientated toward it, it is only to regard it as itself an essence *esse ut significatum*. This error, which may be termed Platonic or Scotist, facilitates the confusion between the metaphysician's being and the logician's.

13. As a result of all these errors the being which is the distinctive object of metaphysics is confused not only with the genuine being of logic, that being we have termed *being divested of reality*, but with the being which is the object of a false logic, a decadent logic, with being as the supreme genus and a pure form of thought. And this being I call *pseudo-being*.

Dialectics

14. I will call your attention to an extremely suggestive fact. Read in the fourth lecture of St. Thomas' Commentary on Book IV of the *Metaphysics* what he tells us of dialectics in the old sense of the term. For by dialectics the ancients understood the science of probable conclusions. It was a portion of logic.[6]

[6] In Met., IV, lec. 4, ed. Cathala 573 ff. "Conveniunt autem in hoc (dialectica et philosophia), quod dialectici est considerare de omnibus. Hoc autem esse non posset, nisi consideraret omnia secundum quod in aliquo uno conveniunt: quia unius scientiae unum subjectum est, et unius artis una est materia, circa quam operatur. Cum igitur omnes res non conveniant nisi in ente, manifestum est quod dialecticae materia est ens, et ea quae sunt entis, de quibus etiam philosophus considerat...

"Differunt autem ab invicem. Philosophus quidem a dialectico secundum potestatem. Nam majoris virtutis est consideratio philosophi quam consideratio dialectici. Philosophus enim de praedictis communibus procedit demonstrative. Et ideo ejus est habere scientiam de praedictis, et est cognoscitivus eorum per certitudinem. Nam certa cognitio sive scientia est effectus demonstrationis. Dialecticus autem circa omnia praedicta procedit ex probabilibus; unde non facit scientiam, sed quamdam opinionem. Et hoc ideo est, quia ens est duplex: ens scilicet rationis et ens naturae. Ens autem rationis dicitur proprie de illis intentionibus, quas ratio adinvenit in rebus consideratis; sicut intentiones generis, speciei et similium, quae quidem non

St. Thomas explains that, like the metaphysician, the dialectician studies all things, which he could not do unless they all possessed a character in common. For science has a single subject matter. Since being alone is common to all things, it is plain that being is the subject matter of dialectic, *ens et quae sunt entis de quibus etiam philosophus considerat.* Here St. Thomas states plainly what I have just been explaining: there is a being which is not the specific object of metaphysics, but the object or rather the subject matter of dialectic so that "the philoso-

---

inveniuntur in rerum natura, sed considerationem rationis consequuntur. Et hujusmodi, scilicet ens rationis, est proprie subjectum logicae. Hujusmodi autem intentiones intelligibiles, entibus naturae aequiparantur, eo quod omnia entia naturae sub consideratione rationis cadunt. Et ideo subjectum logicae ad omnia se extendit, de quibus ens naturae praedicatur. Unde concludit, quod subjectum logicae aequiparatur subjecto philosophiae, quod est ens naturae. Philosophus igitur ex principiis ipsius procedit ad probandum ea quae sunt consideranda circa hujusmodi communia accidentia entis. Dialecticus autem procedit ad ea consideranda ex intentionibus rationis, quae sunt extranea a natura rerum. Et ideo dicitur, quod dialectica est tentativa, quia tentare proprium est ex principiis extraneis procedere...

"Licet autem dicatur, quod Philosophia est scientia, non autem dialectica et sophistica, non tamen per hoc removetur quin dialectica et sophistica sint scientiae. Dialectica enim potest considerari secundum quod est docens, et secundum quod est utens. Secundum quidem quod est docens, habet considerationem de istis intentionibus, instituens modum, quo per eas procedi possit ad conclusiones in singulis scientiis probabiliter ostendendas: et hoc demonstrative facit, et secundum hoc est scientia. Utens vero est secundum quod modo adjunctivo utitur ad concludendum aliquid probabiliter in singulis scientiis; et sic recedit a modo scientiae . . .

"Sed in parte logicae quae dicitur demonstrativa, solum doctrina pertinet ad logicam, usus vero ad philosophiam et ad alias particulares scientias quae sunt de rebus naturae. Et hoc ideo, quia usus demonstrativae consistit in utendo principiis rerum, de quibus fit demonstratio, quae ad scientias reales pertinet, non utendo intentionibus logicis. Et sic apparet, quod quaedam partes logicae habent ipsam scientiam et doctrinam et usum, sicut dialectica tentativa et sophistica; quaedam autem doctrinam et non usum, sicut demonstrativa."

pher, the dialectician, and the sophist study" the same thing, namely being. Nevertheless they differ from each other. The philosopher differs from the dialectician in intellectual power, *secundum potestatem*. For his vision is keener and possesses greater force than the dialectician's. In respect indeed of all these objects enveloped in being the philosopher proceeds by demonstration and by ways capable in themselves of producing certainty. The dialectician, on the other hand, proceeds in respect of all these by probable arguments. That is why he never achieves science and must be content with opinion. St. Thomas gives us the clue to all this. "This we say is the case because being is twofold, conceptual being (*ens rationis*) and real being; and conceptual being, that is being which cannot exist outside the mind and must exist in it, is strictly the subject of logic." So the fold is as wide as the material. "The intelligible objects of the logician are co-extensive with real beings, since all real objects enter into the purview of reason. Hence the subject of logic extends to all things that possess reality." The subject matter of logic is co-extensive with the subject matter of philosophy, which is real being. But being is studied as transferred into the intellect and unable to exist outside it. And the procedure of the dialectician is to study objects not by real causes but by conceptual intentions, "that is conceptual beings of a logical nature which are extraneous to reality," *extranea a natura rerum*.

St. Thomas goes on to explain that dialectic can be considered as it belongs to pure or to applied logic, *logica docens* or *logica utens*, as it is taught or employed. As taught it is a science, because it demonstrates to us the procedure by which we reach probability. On the contrary, when it is employed as an intellectual tool, it is the very intellectual procedure which studies objects from the standpoint not of real but of conceptual being, using probable arguments. It is then no longer a science because it produces only opinion. Hence the ancients divided logic into three parts, demonstrative, dialectic, and sophistic logic.

Between these three parts the following difference obtains. In demonstrative logic the *theory* of demonstration, pure logic, *logica docens,* pertains to logic. But the practice or employment of demonstration, applied logic, *logica utens,* is not the concern of the logician but of every man who studies reality. In the case of dialectical logic, and it is the same with sophistic, both employment and instruction, practice as well as theory, are the logician's province. To know objects not in accordance with their real structure, but in accordance with the ideal structure of our conceptual beings and therefore in a fashion confined of its very nature to the probable, is the logician's task, as it is also his task to construct the theory of probable reasoning. It is not the task of the natural philosopher or of the metaphysician.

If you bear in mind St. Thomas' description of dialectic and the dialectician you will observe that the term dialectic as employed by modern philosophers has undoubtedly a different meaning. It now designates a procedure which passes from opposites to opposites to engender reality, starting from the most primitive notion. But the very name is extraordinarily revealing. It informs us, reveals, *admits* that the philosophies in question are not the work of a genuine philosopher but of a logician, that is to say that their authors studied objects and attempted to explain them not by real causes but by conceptual beings, that is from the standpoint of the logical *ens rationis.* They sought a *logical* explanation of things, and in saying this I stress the term logic inasmuch as logic is the science of conceptual being and not a science of real being. The genuine philosopher, however, seeks an *ontological* (metalogical) explanation of things and is not content with a merely logical explanation.

Here we must break off. You will notice that what we have first encountered on our way are forms of being which are not the being which is the subject matter of metaphysics but, insofar as they claim to be so, are but counterfeits of it, namely the *particularized* being of the sciences inferior to metaphysics, the *vague* being of common sense, the being *divested of reality* which is the subject of logic, and the *pseudo-being* of a misconceived and decadent logic.

In the next lecture I shall speak of the being which is the genuine subject matter of metaphysics. It will be easier to distinguish now that we have seen other meanings of the term being with which it might be confused. ✎

THIRD LECTURE

The True Subject of Metaphysics

I. The Intuition of Being as Such

1. In my last lesson I began to deal with the subject matter of metaphysics, namely being as such, *ens secundum quod est ens*. And the better to distinguish it and its distinctive characteristics I found it profitable to consider first a number of aspects under which being may be presented to our intellect but which are not the aspect we are looking for. So I pointed out cursorily four kinds of "being" which are not the genuine object of the metaphysician.

I have now to deal with being insofar as being, *ens in quantum ens*. This is the ultimate object to be attained by the intellect, which it attains at the summit of its natural knowledge. It boxes the compass. For it sets out from being, but from being as it is immediately apprehended when the mind first awakes in the sensible world. That is its starting point. And at the end of its course it arrives at being, but being envisaged in itself, disengaged from its matrix, viewed in its own light and in accordance with its own type of intelligibility. The last lecture will have shown you that it is an intellectual disaster to confound this "being" which is the subject matter of metaphysics with any one of those kinds of being I then pointed out to you. Otherwise we should find ourselves obliged—particularly if we stopped short at the being which is the subject matter of logic or at what I termed pseudo-being and supposed that it is to this being, or pseudo-being, that the metaphysician ascribes real value—to regard being as but a by-product of language, in which case the philosopher would indeed "vanish in his thoughts."

The being which is the subject matter of metaphysics, being as such, is neither the particularized being of the natural sciences, nor the being divested of reality of genuine logic, nor yet the pseudo-being of false logic. It is real being in all the purity and fullness of its distinctive intelligibility—or mystery. Objects, all objects, murmur this being; they utter it to the intellect, but not to all intellects, only to those capable of hearing. For here also it is true: He that hath ears to hear let him hear. *Qui habet aures audiendi audiat.* Being is then seen in its distinctive properties, as transobjectively subsistent, autonomous, and essentially diversified. For the intuition of being is also the intuition of its transcendental character and analogical value. It is not enough to employ the word being, to say "being." We must have the intuition, the intellectual perception of the inexhaustible and incomprehensible reality thus manifested as the object of this perception. It is this intuition that makes the metaphysician.

2. As you know, to each science there belongs a distinctive intellectual virtue. There is, therefore, an intellectual virtue proper to the metaphysician. And this virtue, or habitus, corresponds to being as the object of the intuition just mentioned. We must therefore distinguish two "lights" in scholastic parlance, one pertaining to the object, the other to the habitus, or intellectual virtue. The characteristic mode of intellectual apprehen-

sion or eidetic visualization—the degree of immateriality, of spirituality in the manner in which the mind grasps the object and conforms to it, demanded by the very nature of transobjective reality as it presents to the mind as its object a particular intelligible facet—constitutes what the ancients termed the *ratio formalis sub qua*, the objective light in which at a given degree of knowledge objects are knowable by the intellect. At the same time, proportionate to this objective light there is a subjective light perfecting the subjective activity of the intellect, by which the intellect itself is proportioned to a given object, fitted to apprehend it. That is why Thomists say that the habitus is a *lumen*, a light, not in the objective but in the *effective* order. For it is concerned with the production or effectuation of the act of knowing.

Hence the metaphysical habitus is requisite, if we are to have the intuition of being as such, *ens in quantum ens.* Yet on the other hand it is this intuition that effects, causes, the metaphysical habitus. This reciprocal causation simply means that the metaphysical habitus, the intellectual virtue of the metaphysician, comes to birth at the same time as its proper and specific object is disclosed to it. Nevertheless the object is prior, not in time but in ontological rank. In the order of nature the intuition of being as such takes precedence of the inner habitus of the metaphysician. It is this perception of being that determines the first moment at which the habitus comes to birth, and it is by the operation of this same habit thus developed that the being which is the metaphysician's distinctive object is more and more clearly perceived.

3. Enough of this digression. We are confronted here with a genuine intuition, a perception direct and immediate, an intuition not in the technical sense which the ancients attached to the term, but in the sense we may accept from modern philosophy. It is a very simple sight, superior to any discursive reasoning or demonstration, because it is the source of demonstration. It is a sight whose content and implications no words of human speech

can exhaust or adequately express and in which in a moment of decisive emotion, as it were, of spiritual conflagration, the soul is in contact, a living, penetrating, and illuminating contact, with a reality which it touches and which takes hold of it. Now what I want to emphasize is that it is being more than anything else which produces such an intuition. The characteristics of intuition as I have just described them may seem at first sight those of M. Bergson's intuition. They seem so, in truth, but with the important difference that he denies that his intuition is intellectual. I, on the other hand, have just maintained that the object par excellence of intuition is being, but that that intuition is intellectual. This is remote indeed from the Bergsonian philosophy. Being does not produce the intuition such as I have described it, by means of that species of sympathy which demands a violent return of the will upon itself, of which M. Bergson speaks, but evokes it from the intellect and by means of a concept, an idea. The concept, or notion, of being corresponds with this intuition. The term being is the correct term to express it, though obviously we cannot display by this poor word nor for that matter by the most skillful devices of language all the wealth contained in the intuition. It requires all the metaphysics hitherto elaborated or to be elaborated hereafter in its entire future development to know all the riches implicit in the concept of being. It is by producing in conjunction with reality a mental word within itself that the intellect immediately attains being as such, the subject matter of metaphysics.

Thus we are confronted with objects, and as we confront them, the diverse realities made known by our senses or by the several sciences, we receive at a given moment, as it were, the revelation of an intelligible mystery concealed in them. Nor is this revelation, this species of intellectual shock, confined to metaphysicians. It is sometimes given to those who are not metaphysicians. There is a kind of sudden intuition which a soul may receive of her own existence, or of "being" embodied in all things whatsoever, however lowly. It may even happen that to a particular soul this intellectual perception presents the semblance of a mystical grace. I have quoted elsewhere (*Degrés du Savior*, p. 552) a personal experience communicated to me.

"I have often experienced in a sudden intuition the reality of my being, the profound first principle which makes me exist outside nonentity. It is a powerful intuition whose violence has sometimes frightened me and which first revealed to me a metaphysical absolute."

A similar intuition is described in the autobiography of Jean-Paul Richter. "One morning when I was still a child, I was standing on the threshold of the house and looking to my left in the direction of the woodpile when suddenly there came to me from heaven like a lightning flash the thought: I *am a self*, a thought which has never since left me. I perceived my self for the first time and for good."

There are, therefore, metaphysical intuitions which are a natural revelation to the soul, invested with the decisive, imperious, and dominant character of a "substantial word" uttered by reality. They reveal the intelligible treasure, the unforgettable transobjective fact, which is either her own subsistence, the "Self" that she is, or being either her own or the being apprehended in objects. Evidently this intuition of which I am speaking does not necessarily present this appearance of a species of mystical grace. But it is always, so to speak, a gift bestowed upon the intellect, and beyond question it is in one form or another indispensable to every metaphysician. But we must also observe that although it is indispensable to the metaphysician, it is not given to everybody, nor to all those who engage in philosophy, nor even to all philosophers who desire to be or are believed to be metaphysicians. Kant never had it. What is the explanation of this? That it is difficult. It is not indeed difficult like an operation which it is hard to perform, whose successful performance demands expert skill. For there is nothing simpler. It was precisely because he sought it by a technique, an intellectual technique of extreme sublety, that Kant failed to attain it.

Moreover, it is as true to say that this intuition produces itself through the medium of the vital action of our intellect, I mean as vitally receptive and contemplative, as to say that we produce it. It is difficult, inasmuch as it is difficult to arrive at the degree of intellectual purification at which this act is produced in us, at which we become sufficiently disengaged, sufficiently empty to *hear* what all things whisper and to *listen* instead of composing answers.

We must attain a certain level of intellectual spirituality, such that the impact of reality upon the intellect—or to use a less crude metaphor, the active, attentive silence of the intellect, its meeting with the real—gives the objects received through our senses (whose *species impressa* is buried in the depths of the intellect) a new kind of presence in us: they are present in a mental word, another life, a living content which is a world of transobjective presence and intelligibility. Then we are confronted within ourselves with the object of this intuition, as an object of knowledge, living with an immaterial life, with the burning translucence of intellectual nature in act.

II. *Concrete Approaches To This Intuition*

4. It is worth remarking at this point that there are concrete approaches which prepare for this intuition and lead up to it. They are different *paths* which, however, it is important to observe, are radically insufficient if we stop short at them, but which may prove useful to particular individuals if they will transcend them, if they will go further. Here I will mention three of these. One is the Bergsonian experience of duration. Within limits it is a genuine experience.

Duration is apprehended by an experience of motion in which, on a level deeper than that of consciousness, our psychic states fuse in a potential manifold which is, notwithstanding, a unity, and in which we are aware of advancing through time and enduring through change indivisibly, yet that we are growing richer in quality and triumphing over the inertia of matter. This is a psychological experience which is not yet the metaphysical intuition of being, but is capable of leading us up to it. For involved in this psychological duration and implicitly given by it there is indeed existence, the irreducible value of being, *esse*.

This intuition is therefore a path, an approach, to the perception of existence. The latter, however, is not yet nakedly displayed in its own intelligible form.

5. The German philosopher, Heidegger, assures us that no man can become a metaphysician who has not first experienced anguish, this anguish being understood not only psychologically but also as metaphysically as possible. It is the feeling at once keen and lacerating of all that is precarious and imperiled in our existence, in human existence. As the effect of this feeling, of this anguish, our existence loses its commonplace and acquires a unique value, its unique value. It confronts us as something saved from nothingness, snatched from nonentity.

Certainly such a dramatic experience of nothingness may serve as an introduction to the intuition of being, provided it is taken as no more than an introduction.

6. My third example is not a thesis fully worked out, but suggestions put forward in preliminary sketches or in the course of conversation. Therefore I must speak of it with all due reserve and without committing its author to my interpretation. It would seem that M. Gabriel Marcel is seeking a method of approach to metaphysical being by deepening the sense of certain moral facts, such as fidelity. As Heidegger attaches himself to a personal experience, a psychological experience such as anguish, while warning us that he is not concerned with psychology, so the notion of fidelity is here understood in a sense which does or should transcend ethics and con-

veys strictly metaphysical value and content. We may observe that the consistency, *steadfastness*, firmness, and victory over disintegration and oblivion contained in this virtue and suggested by the word fidelity are strictly dependent upon a certain *steadfastness* in reality itself in virtue of which I dominate the flux of my own life and possess my metaphysical consistence. Therefore, if I rightly understand M. Marcel's thought, if we follow its direction we shall conclude that a philosophy of life which confuses my *self* with the flux of my life in inconsistent with the experience of fidelity. The experience, the irreducible reality of what I experience and know as fidelity, is pregnant with an ontological realism.

These Approaches Are Useful Only If We Take the Decisive Step

7. In these three instances we are, you see, confronted with so many concrete approaches to being. The first of these experiences, that of duration, belongs to the speculative order, and is at once psychological and biological. The two others belong to the practical and moral order, the psychological factor being invested with the ethical. If we stop here, we have not, I maintain, crossed the threshold of metaphysics. These philosophic explorations are certainly not to be despised or refused. They can perform most valuable service by directing toward being many minds hidebound by idealist prejudices or repelled by some textbook of so-called scholasticism. They can prepare them to recover the sense of being. But they can do this only if we will travel further; cross the threshold, take the decisive step. Otherwise, whatever we do, we shall remain in psychology and ethics, which we shall then work up, swell out, enlarge or rarefy to make them mimic metaphysics. We shall then have, not genuine metaphysics, but a substitute which may certainly possess a very considerable philosophic interest,

but is nothing but a substitute all the same. The utmost that can be achieved along these lines are solutions obtained by an indirect route which skirts the essential issue or by definitions based on external criteria, not the genuine solutions demanded by a science worthy of the name, by philosophic knowledge. Even if psychology and ethics enrich their own speech with metaphysical echoes or undertones, they will be but echoes.

But the most serious danger which all these methods of approaching being involve is the danger of remaining imprisoned in one or other of the concrete analogues of being, whichever one has chosen as a path to it. The experience in question gives information only of itself. This is indeed the drawback of pure experience in philosophy and the pitfall of every metaphysical system which attempts to be empirical. The experience, though valid for the domain covered by the particular intuition, cannot, save by an arbitrary procedure, be extended to a wider province of the intelligible world, and be employed to explain it. On the other hand, as I have just said, such experiences bring us to the threshold which it is then for us to cross by taking the decisive step. We do this by letting the veils—too heavy with matter and too opaque —of the concrete psychological or ethical fact fall away to discover in their purity the strictly metaphysical values which such experiences concealed. There is then but one word by which we can express our discovery, namely being. Let us have the courage to require our intellect, acting as such, to look the reality signified by the term in the face. It is something primordial, at once very simple and very rich and, if you will, inexpressible in the sense that is it that whose perception is the most difficult to describe, because it is the most immediate. Here we are at the root, at last laid bare, of our entire intellectual life. You may say, if you please, for I am here attempting to employ a purely descriptive terminology as a preliminary to the formation of a philosophic vocabulary, that what is now perceived is, as it were, a pure activity, a subsistence, but a subsistence which transcends the entire order of the imaginable, a living

tenacity, at once precarious—it is nothing for me to crush
a fly—and indomitable—within and around me there is
growth without ceasing. By this subsistence, this tenacity,
objects come up against me, overcome possible disaster,
endure and possess in themselves whatever is requisite
for this. These are metaphors, lamentably inadequate,
which attempt to express not so much what my intellect
sees, which is super-empirical, as my experience of the
vision, and do not themselves enter the domain of metaphysics but which may make us aware that to the word
"being," when it expresses a genuine metaphysical intuition, there must correspond a primary and original
datum, of its essence above the scope of observation.

So true is it that the words "being," "existence," are
pregnant with a metaphysical content which transcends
observation, that, in order to free us from it, logical
empiricists have proposed to abandon the term "existence." It is a bold though impossible solution, and moreover entirely consistent with the principles of empiricism,
inasmuch as they demand the formation of a philosophic
vocabulary completely divested of ontological reference.
In the *Revue de Métaphysique et de Morale* (April–
June, 1931) I read an article by Madame Christine Ladd-
Franklin, entitled *La Non-Existence de l'Existence,* in
which she proposes, in order to satisfy the demands of a
scientific method devoid of ontology, in fact, of a purely
empirical metaphysic, to substitute for the word "existence" the phrase "*event* in such and such a province of
thought."

This metaphysical content, of which we are speaking,
covers the entire domain of intelligibility and reality.
It is a gift bestowed upon the intellect by an intuition
which infinitely exceeds, I do not say in the intensity of
its experience but in its intelligible value, the experiences
which may have led up to it.

III. Confirmatory Rational Analysis

8. I have spoken briefly of the intuition of being and of the paths which may lead to its threshold. I must add that it is both possible and necessary to show analytically that to arrive at this point is inevitable. We are now dealing with something totally different from those concrete approaches to being which I have just discussed. We are now concerned with a rational analysis establishing the necessity of being as such, *ens in quantum ens*, as the supreme object of our knowledge. Such an analytic proof presupposes, as taken for granted by common sense or as scientifically confirmed by the criticism of knowledge, what in general terms we may call the objective or rather transobjective validity of understanding and knowledge, a nonidealist position. It is then easy to prove that it is only in appearance that we can dispense, as Madame Ladd-Franklin would have us do, with the notions of being and existence, even though we speak of "event" and attempt to prove that we should substitute this choicer term for the word existence. The entire series of concepts employed to reach her conclusion witnesses at every turn the primacy of the notion of being. It is argued, for example, that philosophers who employ the term existence *are mistaken* and that a sound scientific method *requires* the abandonment of ontological notions. But being is still there—not always the word, but the object which it signifies. And at every turn the critic makes use, unawares, of this intelligible value of being, which it is claimed has been got rid of. Every attempt to eliminate the notion of being refutes itself.

In the second place it is easy to prove, as St. Thomas proves in the first article of his *De Veritate,* that all our notions, all our concepts, are resolved in the concept of being. It is therefore the first of all our concepts, of which all the rest are determinations. Being is determined by the differences which arise within, not outside, itself. It is then to being that we inevitably reascend as to the fountainhead. It is being which the intellect perceives first and before anything else. It is, therefore, being which the metaphysical intellect must disengage and know in its distinctive mystery. On this point consult the texts of the *Metaphysics* mentioned in my last lecture.

9. It is, however, important to observe that the intuition of which I was speaking just now and the analysis with which I am at present concerned should accompany each other. Were we content with the intuition without the rational analysis we should risk being landed with an intuition unconfirmed by reason, whose rational necessity therefore would not be manifest. Were we content with the analysis—as we are liable to be when we teach philosophy—though the analysis would indeed prove that we must arrive at the intuition of being as the goal of a necessary regress, it would not of itself furnish the intuition. Thus the analysis is in the same case as the approaches of which I spoke earlier. The latter led up concretely, *in via inventionis,* to the metaphysical intuition of being. But it still remained to cross the threshold to which they had led us. It is the same with rational analysis. It leads us by logical necessity, and *in via judicii,* to the threshold which an intuitive perception alone enables us to cross, the perception of being as such. When the mind once has this intuition it has it for good.

Observe what an unforgettable event in the history of philosophy was Parmenides' discovery, imperfect though it still was, of being as such. It was on that account that Plato called him the father of philosophy, and when obliged to criticize him accused himself of parricide. Parmenides was, it would seem, the first Western philosopher to have the perception, though still very imperfect as I have said, of being as such. It was imperfect, for he does not seem to have disengaged it in its naked metaphysical value. He appears, as his theory of the sphere indicates, to have amalgamated the metaphysical intuition of being with a physical perception of sensible reality and to have misunderstood or misinterpreted his intuition of being, when the inevitable moment arrived for him to explain it in terms of philosophic concepts, by understanding it univocally and thus falling into monism.

You will also see why the intuition of the principle of identity, every being is what it is, being is being, can possess such value for the metaphysician, can become the object of his enraptured contemplation. Common sense—and therefore the man in the street—makes use of the principle without scrutinizing it. "A cat is a cat," says common sense—what more could it say?—so that, if the philosopher comes on the scene and enunciates the principle of identity in front of common sense, the latter will not *see* it, but will merely have the impression that an insignificant commonplace has been affirmed, in fact a tautology. The philosopher, on the other hand, when he enunciates the principle of identity, enunciates it as an expression of the metaphysical intuition of being, and thus sees in it the first fundamental law of reality itself, a law which astounds him because it proclaims *ex abrupto* the primal mystery of being, its combination of subsistence and abundance, a law which is exemplified by objects in an infinite number of different modes, and applied with an infinite variety. It is not as the result of a logistic process that the metaphysician perceives and employs the principle of identity, so that it compels him to reduce everything to a pure identity, that is to say, to obliterate all the diversities and varieties of being. For it is with its mode of analogical realization that he apprehends the principle. When he apprehends being as such, being according to its pure intelligible nature, he apprehends the essentially analogous value of the concept of being which is implicitly manifold and is realized in diverse objects in such fashion as to admit differences of essence between them, complete and vast differences. The principle of identity secures the multiplicity and variety of objects. Far from reducing all things to identity, it is, as I have explained elsewhere, the guardian of universal multiplicity, the axiom of being's irreducible diversities. If each being is what it is, it is not what other beings are.

The Intuition of Being as Such Is an Eidetic Intuition

10. It follows that the metaphysical intuition of being is an abstractive intuition. Abstraction, however, is an antique term rendered suspect to modern ears by the distortion of long use and by errors and misconceptions of every sort. Therefore instead of *abstraction* I propose to speak of *eidetic or ideating visualization.* I maintain then that the metaphysical intuition of being is an ideating intuition, that is an intuition producing an idea, and this in a pre-eminent degree. How could it be otherwise with the pure speculative operation of our human intellect? This intuition is at the summit of eidetic intellectuality. What do I mean by the phrase eidetic visualization, *abstractio?* I mean that the intellect by the very fact that it is spiritual proportions its objects to itself, by elevating them within itself to diverse degrees, increasingly pure, of spirituality and immateriality. It is within itself that it attains reality, stripped of its real existence outside the mind and disclosing, uttering in the mind a content, an interior, an intelligible sound or voice, which can possess only in the mind the conditions of its existence one and universal, an existence of intelligibility in act. If being were the object of a concrete intuition like that of an external sense or of introspection, of an intuition centered upon a reality grasped concretely in its singular existence, philosophy would be compelled to choose, as it gave this intuition an idealist or a realist value, between a pure ontological monism and a pure phenomenalist pluralism. If, however, being is, as I have said, analogous, and if the principle of identity

is the axiom of reality's irreducible diversities, it is because extramental being is perceived in the mind under the conditions of the eidetic existence which it receives there, and the imperfect and relative unity it possesses in the mind must be broken up, as also must be the pure and unqualified unity of the objects of univocal concepts, when we pass from its existence in the concept to its real existence. The higher degree in which the intuition of being as such "ideates" is precisely the condition and guarantee of its correct metaphysical employment.

At this point a gulf yawns between the scholastics and many modern philosophers of realist tendencies who attempt to construct an "existential" philosophy and ontology. For many modern philosophers being is indeed the object of an intuition and a decisive encounter,[1] but of

[1] In the study to which I referred above M. Gabriel Marcel (page 8, note 1) employs the term *recollection* and rejects the term *intuition*. An intuition of being, he writes, would be "incapable of taking its place in a collection, of being catalogued as an experience or *Erlebnis* of any kind. For such an experience is always, on the contrary, such that it can be at one instant integrated in its psychological matrix, at the next isolated and, as it were, exposed. Hence any attempt to recall the intuition, to describe it, shall I say, must be fruitless. Therefore to speak of an intuition of being is to invite us to play on a muted piano. This intuition cannot be brought into the light of day, for the simple reason that it is not, in fact, possessed."

In my opinion this passage calls for the following comments:

(1) The metaphysical intuition of being cannot take its place in a collection of repertory of experiences like any experience, or *Erlebnis*, you can think of because it is more fundamental and more immediate than all the rest and relates to a *primary* reality already present in our entire intellectual life.

(2) Nevertheless it is an intuition. It is not indeed "just any intuition or *Erlebnis*" for it is super-empirical. It is a formal intuition, an intellectual perception, the intuition par excellence, of which the human intellect is capable only at the summit of its intellectuality. And for that very reason, because of this presence within itself which is distinctive of what is spiritual, the intellect is able to return upon this direct intuition, an immediate return or reapprehension which is totally different from a recollection or recreation of the past and by which this intuition is "possessed" in its own spiritual light and "dis-

an empirical intuition and a concrete encounter, which however profound, mysterious, and secret it may be supposed to be, always remains of the same nature as those procured by psychological or moral experience. It discovers a singular reality or presence actually existing and acting—in any case a reality which the intellect does not grasp by an eidetic visualization in the transparence of

---

covered" to consciousness which it fills with its music. In this sense to deny the metaphysical intuition of being precisely as an intuition is indeed to invite us to play, on a muted piano, the fundamental harmonies of metaphysics.

(3) If a philosopher who is powerfully aware of the ontological mystery nevertheless is convinced that it cannot be an intuition, it is because idealistic prepossessions do not suffer him to address himself to his intellect as such, and trust to it to satisfy his search. We cannot but see in this attitude the effect of an unsurmounted prejudice against the objectivity of the intellect, which is conceived idealistically. In consequence of this prejudice he will seek to make contact with the ontological mystery, so to speak, by a circuitous route which leads through the subjective domain, therefore specifically by way of the obscure apprehension of love, and thus skirts the object we term being. This object, however, is not a screen, it is being itself. Therefore love does not really skirt it but enters it after its fashion, as does intellect after its own. On the "other side" of it there is only nothingness.

(4) Aristotle observed that metaphysics is too lofty for us to possess securely. It is only with a precarious grasp that the metaphysical intuition of being is "possessed" in that awareness of which I spoke just now. On the one hand its object is supremely inexhaustible, and is presented to us as such; on the other hand this intuition, with the awareness that reduplicates it, far from being always in act becomes habitual. We actualize it at will but in a fashion usually imperfect and without recapturing the original vividness, though it is also true that we can make it indefinitely deeper and more intense.

I would add that "the assurance which underlies the entire process of thought, even discursive" of which M. Gabriel Marcel rightly speaks, belongs, in fact, to the obscure intuition of being possessed by common sense, the perception of what I have termed vague being. It is only when the metaphysical intuition of being has occurred that this assurance refers to it also. It is then confirmed, strengthened, and made selfconscious.

an idea or concept. And it discovers it by a kind of affective and experienced connaturality.

It is therefore an idealist prejudice which prevents these philosophers from making a frank and deliberate use of the eidetic intuition. They fail to see that they do employ it all the same but on its lowest level and mingled with sensible and emotional factors, the level, namely, of psychological experience or experiences even more enveloped by the opacity of the senses.

Hence, although the various forms of experience of which I have been speaking may serve as paths to the metaphysical perception of being, they cannot of themselves constitute it. This perception, this intuition is of supremely eidetic order, is purely intelligible, not empirical. That is the reason why many who think themselves metaphysicians are in fact psychologists or moral philosophers, and though striving to reach metaphysics, mimic rather than attain the perception of which I am speaking.

Thomism, as I have already observed, merits the appellation of an existential philosophy, and this already in the speculative order, in what concerns the speculative portion of philosophy. But though Thomist metaphysics is an existential metaphysics, it is so by being and remaining metaphysics, a wisdom whose procedure is intellectual and in strict accordance with the demands of the intellect and its distinctive intuitiveness.

FOURTH LECTURE

CONSIDERATIONS ABOUT BEING AS SUCH

1. The Analogy of Being

1. I have spoken of the intuition of being precisely as the subject matter of metaphysics, of being as such, and of the concrete approaches to that intuition, also of the rational analysis which demands it by proving retrogressively that being is our first and indispensable object of thought. I have further observed that this intuition, taken as an *experience* lived by myself, that is from the side of the subject, is like every experience unutterable, or rather more so than any other experience, and therefore can be described or suggested only approximately. In this respect we can speak of an intelligible "revelation," and say that an intellectual perception invested with a more or less intense emotional atmosphere suddenly confronts us with this extraordinary and "unimaginable" reality which has risen up, as it were, for the first time before the eyes of the mind. As a result of this perception, it is evident that I myself and all things are subsistent and determinate, snatched from nonentity, loss, disaster, maintained, and maintaining ourselves, outside it.

The *object,* however, to which this intellectual intuition relates can perfectly well be named, is by no means unutterable. It is, on the contrary, the first object to be conceived. I have in fact conceived it as embodied in sensible objects long before I conceived it, as I now do, in itself. From childhood I have given it a name. It is perceived in a mental word which we express by the term being, and cannot express otherwise. Being, existence, I do not depart from it. If I am asked about this concept of being, called upon to explain it, I shall say and can only say—and this is not a definition but a simple designation—that being is "that which exists or can exist." And this designation possesses meaning only because it thus refers to a primary intuition.

2. This, however, is not the primitive intuition of man as man, but the metaphysician's intuition in which being is beheld in itself and in its essential properties, *secundum quod est ens.* I see it as an intelligible reality which issues from the least thing and in diverse respects belongs to all things. It is as though on opening a bud there came out something bigger than the world, something that, with values and in ways essentially diverse, belongs to the bud in which I saw it first, to my self and to the very Cause of everything which exists. This being as such, the distinctive object of the metaphysician, is, however, grasped by a pure and genuine intuition only when its polyvalence or analogy, its essentially analogous value, is grasped at the same time.

It is a reality independent of myself, which constitutes, thus considered in itself, an entire universe of possible knowledge and intelligibility, of intelligible mystery, and which is not *one* thing, purely and simply one, but which is everywhere found in essentially different forms. We are thus in a sphere where no sensible image avails anything, neither that of a body which is one purely and simply, nor that of a manifold of visible objects, which are an aggregate without unity. Its subsistence is purely intelligible, and far from excluding, requires its multiplicity and diversification. We might speak of it as a liquid crystal which is the environment of the metaphysical intellect. Being presents me with an infinite intelligible variety which is the diversification of something which I can nevertheless call by one and the same name. It is something that I find everywhere and call by the same name, because it is in all cases made known to me by the similar relationship which the most diverse objects possess to a certain term essentially diverse, designated in each by our concept of being, as being present formally and intrinsically in it. And this analogical character, an example of what is called the analogy of strict proportionality, is inscribed in the very nature of the concept of being. It is analogous from the outset, not a univocal concept afterward employed analogously. It is essentially analogous, polyvalent. In itself it is but a simple unity of proportionality, that is, it is purely and simply manifold and one in a particular respect.

Essence and Existence

3. I will attempt to bring out more clearly the intelligible subsistence contained in this the first object grasped by the metaphysician's intuition. We are immediately aware of this characteristic of it—that when we consider different things there is in each alike a typical relationship between *what* is, that which philosophers term · essence or nature, and its *esse,* or existence. That is to say, this notion of being involves a species of polarity, essence-existence.

A notion of being which completely abstracts from either of these two aspects is impossible. Surely this fact is worth our attention. The concept of being implicitly involves in its analogous or polyvalent unity the division of being into created and uncreated, into substance and accident. For when I reflect upon being I see it divided into typical kinds of being which differ throughout, created and uncreated being, substantial and accidental being. But in virtue of its essential structure the concept of being also includes in itself indissolubly—at every degree of its polyvalence, and whichever kind of being we are considering, throughout its entire extent, the boundless field which it can cover—these two linked and associated members of the pair essence-existence, which the mind cannot *isolate* in separate concepts. Whatever being I may think of, its concept implies this double aspect. Metaphysics teaches us that in God the distinction between essence and existence is a *distinctio rationis,* a purely ideal distinction, but that in all created objects there is a real distinction between them. Thus the idea of being, however imperfect its unity may be, from the very fact of its higher degree of abstraction, possesses, like every idea, though its unity is imperfect and relative, more unity than the reality it signifies. Not only does this identical notion, when it signifies one analogous being, continue to be valid of another totally different. It also permanently unites in our mind, by its multiple and relative unity, realities—namely essence and existence—which outside the mind are really distinct. To this same notion, to the imperfect unity of the concept of being a real diversity in things permanently corresponds, namely that between essence and existence in all creatures. This is the first observation we can formulate.

Being and the Transcendentals

4. When we consider the transcendentals we reach a second conclusion. There is a reality which I attain in the notion of being, in the intuition of being, and which I express by the term being; and it becomes evident that this reality—even as objectively manifested by and in the notion of being—is richer and more pregnant with

intelligible values than the idea of being by itself immediately reveals. By an intrinsic necessity it must in a sense overflow the very idea in which it is objectified.

This is what I mean. You know that metaphysicians recognize a certain number of universal modes of being, as universal as being itself, which are termed transcendentals (*passiones entis*). For example, *unity* is being inasmuch as it is undivided. This is an aspect of being which rises before the mind—namely its internal consistence. Certainly being can be divided. But insofar as it is, it ceases, renounces itself. To the extent to which anything is, it is one. *Truth* is being inasmuch as it confronts intellection, thought; and this is another aspect of being, thus revealed, a new note struck by it. It *answers* to the knowing mind, speaks to it, superabounds in utterance, expresses, manifests a subsistence for thought, a particular intelligibility which is itself. An object is true—that is to say conforms to *what it* thus says itself to thought, to the intelligibility it enunciates—to the extent that it is. What is then manifest is of the nature of an *obligation* attached to being. An *I ought to be* consubstantial with *I am*. Every being ought to be and is, insofar as it is, in conformity with the expression of it which a perfect Knowledge would produce. Then there is *goodness,* transcendental *good*. Good is being inasmuch as it confronts love, the will. This is another epiphany of being. I shall return to it later. Everything is good, metaphysically good. I am not speaking of moral goodness. Everything is good, that is to say, apt to be loved, to be an object of love, to the extent to which it is.

Hence each of these transcendentals is being itself apprehended under a particular aspect. They add nothing real to it. How could they add anything to being? Outside being there is but nonentity. They are, so to speak, a reduplication of being for and in our mind. There is no real distinction between being and unity, between being and truth, between being and good. They are "convertible" notions. The distinction between these different intelligible infinities is merely conceptual, though based on real-ity, a virtual distinction.

You see, then, that of a single reality, of something which is one and the same outside my mind, of something which precisely as being is one, true and good, of this single and unique reality which exists or is capable of existing outside my mind I possess *several* ideas. The idea, the notion, the *ratio,* the concept of being qua idea, differs from the idea of unity, of truth, of goodness or good. I therefore possess many ideas which correspond to a single and identical reality too rich, too fertile to enter my mind by the medium of a single idea, not even this primary idea, the idea of being. We may say that being compels the concept of being to multiply diverse concepts and exceed itself.

Being and Tendency

5. A third consideration relates to the dynamic character of being, the fact that I cannot posit this reality, grasped by my primary intuition of being as such, without at the same time positing a certain *tendency,* a certain inclination. The Thomists repeating St. Thomas' dictum: "Every form is accompanied by an inclination," hold that this is a truth self-evident to anyone who possesses the metaphysical intuition of being.[1]

To affirm being is to affirm inclination or tendency. We are thus confronted with a kind of communicability or superabundance which is an inherent character of being itself, inasmuch as the notion of being, as I have just hinted, exceeds itself and passes over into the notion of *goodness or good.*

In metaphysical good a new order is disclosed, a cer-

---

[1] *Haec propositio, quod ad omnem formam sequitur inclinatio, per se nota est,* John of St. Thomas, *Curs. Phil.* Vives, Vol. III, p. 523—*Omne esse sequitur appetitus.* Cajetan in I, 19, I.

tain *right* to exist consubstantial with *existence*. For good is seen to be, as it were, a justification of being. It asserts a merit. Being is justified in itself—*justificatum in semetipso,* because it is good. Good, I say, asserts a merit—a glory also and a joy. By this I mean that good, as I indicated above, is essentially bound up with love. A good thing is worthy, metaphysically, though, alas, not always morally, to be loved, either in and for itself, as a perfection, with a direct affective love [2]—this is good in the primary sense—or as perfecting something else, with a reflex [3] affective love—this is good in the secondary sense.

The notion of good, like every transcendental notion, is a primary notion, which suddenly enters the field of vision when we look at being from a particular angle, and reveals a new aspect of it, a new intelligible mystery consubstantial with being. This prospect in the depths of being is disclosed, together with the love which it confronts and in relation to which it is defined. An intellect which *per impossible* lacked the notion of love would lack that of good which is correlative to it.

6. I have affirmed that the truth, *ad omnem formam sequitur inclinatio,* or even more generally wherever there is being, there is tendency and love, *omne esse sequitur appetitus,* is evident immediately we perceive that the idea of being passes over of itself into the idea of good, that being overflows in good or goodness. This axiom can be verified in two different ways, on two dis-

[2] I understand by this a love which wills an object in and for itself. Such is the intellect's love of truth, or the upright man's love of "moral good" the *bonum honestum,* or the "love of friendship," we entertain for ourselves or others.

[3] I understand by this a love whose motion is bent, passing from an object it wills to another object, which is loved with a rectilinear love. Such is the love of what is good for use or pleasure, the *bonum utile* and the *bonum delectabile,* or the "love of desire," with which we will a particular good to ourselves or our friends.

tinct planes, as the superabundance of being is regarded in relation to that which superabounds or in relation to that which receives or may receive this superabundance. '

Let us contemplate this aspect of being, metaphysical good in respect of the multitude of different existents (*omnia*). By the very fact that being is good it implies *in all existents* a tendency toward, a desire for this good. That is why the ancients with Aristotle defined good as *id quod omnia appetunt,* what all things, individually and severally, desire. Thus one thing is good for another, and moreover on all the analogical levels. We say that rain is good for vegetables, truth good for the intellect. The correlative desire, whether of the vegetables for the rain or of the intellect for truth, pertains to what the scholastics term *appetitus naturalis,* what we may call "natural," or consubstantial, inclination (appetite). Thus matter desires form or rather forms, and this desire is itself. Only by that desire does it partake of being. We say that food is good for an animal. This desire pertains to the sensible appetite. We say that to enjoy the good opinion of his fellows is good for man, or that a friend's existence is good for the man whose friend he is. The desire for these goods pertains to the intelligent appetite or the will. It is, therefore, in all sorts of ways essentially different that one thing is good for another. And God is good for all things and they desire Him. ˎ

7. The axiom with which we are now occupied can be verified in another and a deeper fashion. The goodness which is coterminous with being endows *being itself* with a tendency to expand and pass beyond itself, to communicate a surplus. Thus we observe in every natural agent belonging to this sensible universe a tendency to perfect another by transitive action or to perfect itself ontologically by the immanent action of the living organism which builds up itself.

At an incommensurably higher degree in the hierarchy of being there is a tendency to overflow in knowledge and in love. And in both cases the subject at the same time perfects itself. This acquisition of a new perfection accompanies in every creature the superabundance of which I am speaking. But it is not *of itself* (*ex vi notionis*) implied by it. Formally it is the superabundance as such which is essential. The superabundance of *knowledge* expresses the perfection of a being which, in a particular fashion, *is;* which is itself or other things in virtue of a supra-subjective existence (which, in all creatures capable of knowing, is an existence of the intentional order). The superabundance of *love* utters the generosity of a being which *tends* in a particular fashion, which overflows toward something, itself or others, in virtue of a supra-subjective existence (which, in all creatures, is an existence of the intentional order)—existence as a gift.

This love of a psychic or spiritual order, such as the love of the intelligence for truth, to which we have already referred, the ancients termed *"amor elicitus"*; we may call it "elicit love"; prior to it there exists in all things a *radical* love—*"amor naturalis"* an ontological tendency indistinguishable from the essence itself, or the powers of the substance in question. It is thus that every being loves itself and God more than itself, by this "natural," or consubstantial appetite which proceeds not from knowledge but from its very substance, and which exists in a stone or a tree as well as in man. Now, when a being knows itself, and can say *ego,* when it possesses in itself by knowledge of its acts and reflection upon them the form of its own being, what it thus possesses in itself according to the intentional being of knowledge is the form of this radical appetite itself, this natural love of itself which is consubstantial with it, and which is now reduplicated by a psychical appetite, an elicited appetite, that is to say an appetite proceeding from knowledge. This love also is a natural love, but now as a movement of the will. In other words, to know myself is to know a good which I already love radically with a consubstantial love, and toward which I henceforth overflow according to the spiritual being of love, thus formally constituting it a subject, I to myself, and drawing all things toward it. I thus love myself naturally with an elicit love which is a love of direct affection, that is of friendship.

And when I know something other than myself, when by knowledge I possess in myself the form of something else, either I have a tendency or affective overflow toward that object which I will because it is good for me, and I produce in myself, as it were, a spiritual weight which draws me toward it that I may incorporate it into myself, that it may be *mine*—this is the love of refracted affection or desire; or I have a tendency or affective overflow toward this object to which I will good because it is good, and I produce in myself a spiritual weight, or impulse, by which I draw all things and myself to this other being which for me becomes an *ego,* a subject, and to which I wish to be in some way or other really united, as to myself. This is the love of direct affection or of friendship.

8. In the first of the three cases we have just considered, the love of friendship for oneself, the being which is its subject certainly tends to perfect himself. But above all he overflows by *giving* himself, so to speak, to himself. In the second case also, the love of desire, the subject tends to perfect himself but in a fashion altogether different from that in which the simple vegetative organism does so. For he wills good to himself. It is no longer a simple biological fact, a building up of self by and in a natural being. It is a case of volition. The subject seeks to obtain for himself a *gift* which proceeds from the will and the *esse amoris,* a superabundance of a higher order. In the third case, love of friendship for another, the subject tends to perfect the other; also, it is true, himself indirectly. He tends to perfect another, but in a fashion totally different from that of natural agents. For in the case of beings endowed with will, of the overflow of a higher kind peculiar to the order of love, it is a condition of the *gift* made to another that the giver has inwardly given himself to the recipient, has in some measure disappropriated himself in his favor, so that he has become another self. It is in

this that the overflow, distinctive of love, essentially consists.

Finally, if the being that loves *is* Himself intellection and love, as God is, when He knows and loves Himself He does not perfect Himself, acquires no new perfection. But He overflows all the same. And this overflow is His being itself. When the creature overflows it perfects itself, its being becomes fuller. In the case of God, on the contrary, there is no growth or perfecting of His Being. But there is always this overflow of intellection and love which constitutes His Being itself, so that there is actually no distinction, not even a virtual distinction, between God's Being and His understanding, or between His Being and His Love. What *formally constitutes* His Nature, so far as we can conceive it, is the act of intellection. But the privilege of God which most astounds our reason, His *Glory,* is the fact that in Him the ultimate and principal overflow—that of whose very nature it is to be an overflow—namely His Love, is identical with His essence and His existence. For God's fundamental love is itself His elicit love and His *esse.* Therefore, from this point of view, when we regard God in the aspect of His glory, subsistent *Love* is His true and most secret Name, as subsistent *intellect* is His true Name when He is regarded in the aspect of His essence taken as such. *Ego sum qui sum—Deus caritas est.*

Being and Motion

9. The fourth point to which I would draw your attention is the fact that the reality which I attain by the idea of *being* thus implies the *motion* which appears incompatible with it. As we have just seen every being involves a tendency. But a tendency is a motion toward the perfection desired, if it is absent. Consequently wherever there is tendency toward a good not already really

conjoined with the subject, as a perfection possessed by it or as a friend united with it by presence and *convivium,* community of living—that is to say, wherever throughout the created universe creatures display tendency and need to perfect themselves in one fashion or another, and above all in the corporeal universe, the metaphysical home of indigence, there is motion, change.

It is not, therefore, enough to observe that the fact of motion forces itself upon the philosopher as an undeniable fact of experience which is apparently incompatible with being as intuitively apprehended by intellect— from this arose the classical conflict between Heraclitus and Parmenides. We must maintain that being itself—the object of metaphysical intuition—because it involves tendency, involves the motion which seems incompatible with it. Being, therefore, must comprehend two levels, that of actual being, being in act, and potential being, being in potency, that is real possibility, real capacity for a particular determination or perfection. It is this distribution of being on two levels which makes possible a metaphysical analysis of motion. But these two levels, act and potency, are themselves essentially analogous. It is analogously that the notions of act and potency are realized in two different objects.

These very brief observations have been designed simply to make you aware of the diversity and riches contained in the primary intuition of being as such. We must now return to what I have termed the eidetic character of the metaphysical intuition of being, to the fact that it is effected by an abstraction, an "ideating" visualization. In this connection several points, I think, need clearing up.

II. *Extensive and Intensive Visualization*

10. I have already spoken of the most important distinction which the ancient drew between *abstractio*

totalis, which I will call extensive visualization, and *abstractio formalis,* which I will call intensive or characterizing and typifying visualization. At first intellectual visualization is as yet only extensive. That is to say, its object is not explicitly the type or essence abstracted by and for itself, in Platonic terminology the supertemporal form in which objects partake. No doubt the essence is there, but contained in the notion after a fashion wholly implicit or blind, as it were hinted, not such that thought can employ or handle it. What the intellect expresses to itself and explicitly visualizes is simply an object of thought, which, as the logician will say when he reflects upon it, is more or less general. Contact has been made with the intelligible order, the order of the universal in general; but nothing more. The first step has been taken by which we leave the world of sensible experience and enter the intellectual world.

This should be followed by a further step, by which we make contact with the order of the *universal type* and *essential* intelligibility and the typical form is explicitly abstracted and laid bare. This step is the *abstractio formalis,* intensive or typifying visualization by which the mind separates from the contingent and material data the essence of an object of knowledge, that which formally constitutes it. This intensive or typifying visualization is the beginning of scientific knowledge, *knowledge* in the strict sense. And it is according to the degree of this abstraction that the sciences differ one from another, so that the object of a higher degree of intensive visualization, for example the object of metaphysical visualization, is not only more universal, commoner—St. Thomas, you may remember, called metaphysics *scientia communis*—but belongs to another order. It represents a form or regulative type perfected, complete in its distinctive intelligibility. It is, I believe, important to emphasize this point. Observe, for instance, that the concept of being as such with which I am now dealing and which is the subject matter of metaphysics is far more universal, far commoner than the concept of substance, quantity, quality, action, in short than any of

Aristotle's predicaments. The question, therefore, arises: Why are the latter studied by logic rather than by metaphysics whereas being, which is commoner, is studied not by logic but by metaphysics, is the object of the supreme science? If the difference between being and the predicaments were merely one of extension, the concept of being would be simply more indeterminate, and there would therefore be no justification for making it the object of a science of reality and, moreover, of the supreme science. It should be studied by logic like the predicaments. But the predicaments are the supreme *genera,* and knowledge is not in the way of acquiring perfection, is not genuine *knowledge* (*scientia*), if it cannot attain the object wholly determined by its own intelligibility. If you know only by the supreme genus a reality peculiar to a species, if for example you know of man only that he is a substance, you know it in an inadequate and indeterminate fashion. If you go no farther you have not yet reached *scientific* knowledge of the reality in question. That is why the ancients regarded the predicaments merely as intellectual tools with which they could begin to know objects. To classify objects in such categories as substance, quality, or quantity is to begin to know them. Thus the study of the supreme *genera* belongs to the science which deals with the means of knowledge, namely logic. It is the concern of the dialectician, the logician. But true scientific knowledge of objects is achieved when we attain them in their specific nature, in their complete intelligibility as objects of a particular kind.

This is a further proof that being is not a genus. Were being a supreme genus, more universal than the predicaments, there would be no reason to make it the object of a science of reality. Being is, however, transcendental and analogous. When we have an intuition of being as such we enter a new intelligible world superior to that of the predicaments, a world with its distinct and typical intelligibility and noetic subsistence and which the metaphysician can explore in all its dimensions without needing a particular knowledge of specific differences.

German metaphysics attaches great importance to the concept of the "concrete universal." Possibly it has in view, defectively suggested, the universal abstracted by intensive or characterizing, as contrasted with extensive, visualization. Perhaps it is thus aiming at being as such with its transcendental and analogous value, its manifold realizations on every level of the intelligible world, as contrasted with the vague being of common sense or with the logician's being, divested, as I have called it, of reality.

The Degrees of Intensive Visualization

11. As we know, the ancients distinguished three fundamental degrees, or three principal orders of intensive visualization, *abstractio formalis,* and metaphysics belongs to the third and highest of these. You will find important explanations of this doctrine in Cajetan's Commentary on *the prima pars* of the Summa, qIa 3.

The subject or object [4] of a science is the subject matter with which it deals—*ens* in the case of metaphysics. What we may term its index of real intelligibility —*ratio formalis objecti ut res,* or *ratio formalis quae* —is a particular aspect, or, more truly, "inspect," under' which the object appears or presents itself, confronts knowledge, a particular perspective in which it discloses its depths, *entitas* in the case of metaphysics.

The formal subject or object of metaphysics is thus *ens sub ratione entitatis,* being with the index value of the real intelligibility of being—being as such.

[4] The scholastics distinguish between the *subject* of a science, the object of which it treats, and its *object,* the conclusions, the truths at which it arrives concerning that object. The distinction may, however, be disregarded for our purposes.

There is, however, an even more precise and a more formal way of characterizing a science, namely, what we may term the objective light—*ratio formalis objecti ut objectum* or *ratio formalis sub qua*—by which the science in question attains its object. I am speaking of a certain characteristic immateriality in the medium of knowledge, the peculiar mode of visualizing and defining it demanded by the object in question if we are to attain and penetrate it. This objective light thus refers especially to the type of visualization or abstraction. In the case of metaphysics it is a visualization in which knowledge is completely immaterialized, that is to say, the object is visualized *sine omni materia.*

What, in this connection, do we mean by matter? It may be defined as that which renders reality under one aspect or another opaque to our knowledge, unexplorable by the mind, a dead weight of incommunicability. For the root of this incommunicability is what philosophers term prime matter.

Consider the ladder which ascends from pure opacity to the supreme transparence. Its lowest rung is the pure opacity of nothingness. The next rung is the opacity of prime matter which is of its own nature impervious to mind, "unknown by itself" precisely because it does not exist by itself, does not exist in isolation but only in virtue of the form. But it communicates with the form which actualizes it. This is a reminder that transparence to mind, communicability, is co-extensive with being. To the extent to which anything is, it is transparent, communicable, it possesses a certain measure of communicability, a diffusiveness, a generosity. In matter this is at its lowest degree, that of *possibility.*

From the first moment of its existence, matter is not alone. It is conjoined with the form, and exists in virtue of it. But inasmuch as it requires position, it is the basis of the individuation of the form and the compound. It thus restricts and confines being to the closest prison and utmost poverty, that of the corporeal individual. Between one being and another whose form is *entirely* absorbed in informing its matter, namely an inanimate being, no other communication is possible than transitive action. This is the second degree of communicability, that of bodies in their material existence. They can communicate only by the modifications which they receive from each other, each of which is bound up with a corresponding loss. At the upper limit, two bodies communicate their natures to each other *by destroying* each other, to exist henceforward only virtually in a third of a different species. This is substantial generation.

The third degree, or rung, in the ladder of ascent is this: communication is now possible as existence in another, in a soul, but only in virtue of the transitive action of one body upon another, I mean upon a sense organ. In this case bodies exist not only with their corporeal existence but also with the mental, the intentional existence which corresponds to sensation. They become objects. But the object taken in the individuating notes due to prime matter is still imprisoned by the conditions imposed *hic et nunc* by the action of the thing on the senses. It communicates itself only in accordance with these material conditions. Its being remains hidden.

A fourth degree corresponds with intellectual knowledge. Communication is possible as existence in another, in a knowing subject, a soul, and now in virtue of an object's being itself, not simply in virtue of its accidental transitive action, but in virtue of what it is. Things now exist with an intentional existence of the intelligible order. But henceforward, and this is the price paid for this advance, the individuating notes bound up with sensible knowledge, which is itself psychophysical, necessarily fall away. We have entered the sphere of intellectual knowledge which for us men, because it is derived from the senses, is of necessity an abstract or visualizing knowledge. But here, too, there are several degrees.

12. At the lowest degree what a corporeal object is confronts the intellect, as we have seen, divested of its material and singular existence in itself, as also of its existence in the senses, this existence, too, being from

one point of view material and singular. It confronts the intellect involved, invested, embodied in all the diverse qualities of the sensible object. Its being as such is not manifest to the intellect, but merely its being invested with all the diverse qualities proper to the sensible world, *caro et ossa* as the ancients called "sensible matter." They said that at the first degree of abstraction the mind abstracts from the "individual matter" but not from the "sensible matter." Hence the knowledge of sensible nature—that is the philosophy of nature and the natural sciences—studies the actions and passions of bodies, the laws of generation and corruption, motion. Its formal object is *ens sub ratione mobilitatis,* being as subject to motion. And its objective light is a type of visualization in which the conditions of contingent singularity which in sensation hide being fall away, but in which the object is seen and defined by the intellect only by reference to the differences perceived by the outer senses, *cum materia sensibili non tamen hac*—with sensible but not individual matter. When the mind considers in this way what things are, there remains *something in corporeal objects which is not seen,* not known, not communicated, which remains incommunicable. That is why we must advance to a second level or degree of visualization.

At this second degree what an object is confronts the intellect divested of its existence in itself, of its existence in the senses and, moreover, of every sensible quality and of all reference to sense perception. And this divestment is effected by the mind, which explores the object more deeply, and in order to overcome the incommunicability which still remains in it, immaterializes it further. Now, what an object is confronts the intellect as it consists in the quantitative structure of a corporeal being, considered in itself or according to the relations of order and measure distinctive of quantity. Quantity is not now studied as a real accident of corporeal substance, but as the common material of entities reconstructed or constructed by the reason. Nevertheless, even when thus idealized it remains something corporeal, continues to bear in itself witness of the matter whence it is derived.

It is what the ancients called "intelligible matter." They said that at the second degree of abstraction the mind abstracts both from "individual and from sensible" but not from "intelligible matter." The object of mathematical knowledge is thus *ens (reale seu rationis), sub ratione quantitatis,* being whether real or conceptual, under the aspect of quantity. We might rather say *quantum sub ratione quantitatis ipsius, seu relationum quantitativorum ordinis et mensurae,* under the aspect of quantity itself or of quantitative relations of order and measure. Its specific objective light—*modus abstrahendi et definiendi cum materia intelligibili tantum,* abstraction and definition with intelligible matter alone—is a type of visualization in which not only are the conditions of singularity removed, but every reference to the perceptions of the outer senses, yet in which the object is seen and defined by the intellect only in reference, direct or indirect, to the possibility of a sensible construction by the intuitive imagination. The "intelligible matter" is displayed apart; but it still hides from us, indeed it now hides more than ever, the intelligible mystery comprised in the real object, and not revealed at the first degree of abstraction, those higher intelligible realities concealed by the "sensible matter," by a type of visualization which fetters intelligibility itself to sense. Deeper than the world of continuity and number there is still in being *something which is not seen,* in corporeal realities something not communicated to the mind.

For this reason we must ascend to a third degree of visualization, namely to what a corporeal object is when divested alike of its existence in itself, of existence in the senses, and of its sensible and quantitative properties; in short, of everything which in a corporeal object proceeds from matter itself and bears witness to its sovereignty over the very constitution of the object. What an object is thus confronts the intellect divested of everything which bears witness to this sovereignty of matter. Now the intelligible mystery which remained in objects uncommunicated to our mind, that in being which is deeper than the intelligibility tied to the perception of the outer senses or the intelligibility tied to imaginative intuition, is laid bare. This is what the ancients meant when they said that, at the degree of metaphysical knowledge the mind abstracts from matter of any kind, that knowledge of the object is wholly emancipated from matter. There is neither "intelligible" nor "sensible" nor "individual matter." We are in the world of being as such, of the transcendentals, of act and potency, of substance and accident, or intellect and will, all of them realities which can exist in immaterial as well as in material objects. Now the intellect sees in material objects realities capable of existing not only in the objects in which it sees them, but also in immaterial subjects themselves, and finally in the transcendent Cause of all things in whom the transcendental notions, being, unity, truth, intellect, will, and the like are realized in a supereminent unity.

The subject of metaphysics is *ens sub ratione entis,* being with the index value of the real intelligibility of being itself. Its objective light—*modus abstrahendi et definiendi sine omni materia*—abstraction and definition without matter of any kind—is a type of intellectual visualization in which not only are the conditions of singularity wanting, but all reference to the perceptions of the outer senses or to a possible construction by the imaginative intuition. The object is seen and defined by the intellect only in reference to the intelligibility of being itself, in other words, in a purely intelligible and immaterial fashion. There is a supreme immateriality in this mode of knowledge, in this kind of contact effected with objects, which is a pure contact—does not Aristotle say that God touches things without being touched by them?—in the *lumen* or *medium* of knowledge, *medium illustratum per abstractionem ab omni materia,* [5] a medium illuminated by abstracting from matter of any kind. And this objective light of a wholly immaterial kind is that which more than anything else gives metaphysics its specific form. There is no objective light better suited to

[5] Cajetan in I, I, 3.

the intelligible mystery, save the divine light itself, the light of faith and theology, which infinitely exceeds that of metaphysics. Nor is there any objective light more *purified* from the sensible or which renders possible an intuition less entangled with emotional, moral, psychological, or sensible experience. Our intellect has no object more profound than being as such, save the Godhead Itself which is the object of faith, theology, and the beatific vision, an object inaccessible to our merely natural powers. And it is an object which transcends the sensible. There is no object which is in itself more elevated above observation and sensible experience. ·

There is thus a series of successive courts of scientific jurisdiction corresponding with successive levels of intelligibility. We must pass from one to another, drop one veil after another, and so ascend to increasingly pure degrees of formal visualization so long as there is still something left to see in the object, something which could not be seen hitherto, because on the level which had been reached it was still hidden, lay beyond the jurisdiction to which appeal was made. We are thus made conscious at once of the indigence and the greatness of the human mind which can enter the being of objects only by gradual stages, by divesting them first of this, then of that, objective determination, of this and that stratum of knowability, sensible first, then intelligible-physical, then intelligible-mathematical which conceals what still awaits our perceiving. For a pure spirit there could be no question of degrees of abstraction or visualization. It would not abstract. It would see everything in an object from within and as involved in its being itself, down to the final determinants of its singularity. The vision of an angel represents a knowledge at once and indivisibly metaphysical, mathematical, and physical, and which even comprises the intellectual equivalent of sense perception. All these things are distinct for us only because we are intellects that derive from material things themselves by means of the senses, the objects on which they feed. To reject abstraction is to refuse humanity.

III. *Ens Absconditum: Hidden Being*

13. From what has just been said it follows that the loftiest and most precious intuition of our intellect, that of being as such, the intuition which produces the supreme science in the natural order, metaphysics, presupposes the highest degree of divestment by abstraction and of intellectual purity, and that it relates to that which is most universal and commonest, namely, that being which ordinary knowledge does not grasp and disclose in itself, but which is nevertheless its most ordinary tool and, so to speak, its most commonplace material, a material *absolutely* common because it is *always* present. A comparison suggested in a previous lecture recurs to the mind now, namely people with whom we are on very familiar terms but whom it has never occurred to us to look at in their profound and intimate personality. It is the same with being. You understand what is meant by the term abstraction. It must never be separated from the intuition which it effects. That is why in many cases I prefer the term *visualization*.

To abstract means to disengage, to draw out. There is always *something to be disengaged,* a metal from the ore in which it is contained. But we often insist too exclusively upon the negative aspect of the process, the aspect implied by the term abstraction, on the divestment it involves, and fail to see that this divestment is simply a condition. So the term is understood in a purely material fashion, and it becomes incomprehensible how it can designate the supreme degree of human knowledge.

The essence of the process of abstraction, the eidetic visualization, is not to remove baser minerals in which the precious metal is embedded but to find the metal. The essence of metaphysical visualization is not to remove first the individualizing notes, then the sensible qualities, and finally the quantity; it is that of which all this is but the indispensable condition, namely the positive perception, the intuition of being as such. ✓

Far from being a "residue," it is an extremely rich, intelligible substance, living, fresh, and burning, the most efficacious of all, which is thus grasped by the mind. But at the same time, by reason of the abstracting divestment which the purity of such knowledge requires, we can also speak of a certain metaphysical poverty of mind. Precisely because in order to attain this intuition we must discard the mass of too heavy ornaments and strip off the iridescent garments which conceal reality from the metaphysician's gaze, we must remember that the best way of hiding anything is to make it common, to place it among the most ordinary objects. We shall thus understand that the being of metaphysics, the highest and most hidden thing in the natural order, is concealed in the being of common sense. Nothing is more ordinary than being, if we mean the being of everyday knowledge, nothing more hidden, if we mean the being of metaphysics. Like the great saints of poverty it is hidden in light. This, I believe, is a characteristic, a property possessed by all the highest things.

14. If you would like a story which illustrates this truth, recall Poe's tale of "The Purloined Letter." Its subject is a most important letter stolen by a minister in order to compromise an enemy. By a most skillfully conducted inquiry the chief of police attempts to discover the letter. But he fails to do so. For it was hidden in full daylight.

"Yes," said Dupin, "the measures adopted were not only the best of their kind, but carried out to absolute perfection. Had the letter been deposited within the range of their search, these fellows would, beyond a question, have found it."

Similarly if metaphysical being were on the shelf searched by the particular sciences, their methods would most certainly have found it. But it is not there. It is hidden among the most commonplace objects. ✓

This wicked minister had hidden the letter by simply placing it in a card rack against the wall, as though it were the most unimportant trifle. Just because it was in full view it escaped the most meticulous search. Speaking of the minister, Poe explains:

> "*He* could not be so weak as not to see that the most intricate and remote recess of his hotel would be as open as his commonest closets to the eyes, to the probes, to the gimlets and to the microscopes of the Prefect. I saw in fine that he would be driven, as a matter of course, to *simplicity*, if not deliberately induced to it as a matter of choice. You will remember, perhaps, how desperately the Prefect laughed when I suggested upon our first interview that it was just possible this mystery troubled him so much on account of its being so *very* self-evident."

The same thing can be said of the mystery of metaphysical being. It is by reason of its pure simplicity, because it is too simple, almost superhumanly simple, that it eludes philosophers who have not risen to the necessary degree of abstraction and visualization.

Metaphysics, the supreme human science, possesses a characteristic in common with the Gospels. What is most precious and most Divine is hidden under what seems most commonplace. So is it with the Catholic religion in general. There is nothing esoteric about it. It conceals the most precious mysteries under the simplest teaching which it proclaims from the housetops. This, in due proportion, is also true of metaphysics. For the little word "is," the commonest of all words, used every moment everywhere, offers us, though concealed and well concealed, the mystery of being as such. It is from the most ordinary object of common knowledge that the metaphysician educes it, draws it out of its ironical commonplace to look it full in the face. There is, however, a difficulty in this connection of which we should be warned, namely that in an old civilization it is not easy to recover the perceptions prior to language. The triteness of language blunts the mind's power to perceive its significance. With good reason then do we seek to recover a fresher and purer perception, liberated from the routine and mechanism of words. This, in my opinion, is one of the motives of certain contemporary essays in metaphysics. Their authors are seeking this fresh and pure intuition, they are seeking it in defiance of language, therefore as far as possible from *being,* precisely because there is no *word* commoner or in more current use.

It must, however, be sought where it is hidden, and that is precisely in the most ordinary being, expressed by the most commonplace and the tritest of all words.

FIFTH LECTURE

THE PRINCIPLES OF IDENTITY, SUFFICIENT REASON, AND FINALITY

I. An Attempt To Reflect upon the Intuitive Character of First Principles

1. For Thomism there are many first principles. But an order obtains among them. This does not mean that those which come after the first can be demonstrated from it, but that we can prove by a *reductio ad impossibile* that if any of the other first principles of reason is denied you necessarily deny the first, namely the principle of identity, and if the principle of identity is denied you can neither think nor speak, cannot indeed *exist* as a thinking being, as a man.

Nevertheless, I am not going to enter today on this path of *reductio ad absurdum*. I shall invite you, above all, to reflect upon the intuitive character of the first principles. To bring home to ourselves the intuitive value of these first principles of reason it is important to remember what I said in my last lecture about the riches of being, the fact that when this object of thought becomes known to me by and in the notion of being, I am aware

at the same time of its expansive energy. The reality
which I attain in and by my idea of being is, inasmuch as
it becomes objectified in my idea, richer than that idea,
and presses for multiplication in a manifold of notions—
notions of unity, of goodness, of truth. These are transcendental notions. Each of them expresses to the mind
nothing but being itself, to which it adds nothing save a
conceptual difference, a conceptual aspect. In virtue,
however, of precisely this ideal element in which one
differs from another, these notions, as notions, differ
one from another and from the notion of being. They
are convertible but not identical notions, and their names
are not synonyms. Thus there is, as it were, a superflux
of being in respect of our ideas, of the notions in which
it is objectified, and it is in terms of this superflux that I
wish to put before you some brief reflections on the
first principles. We shall try to understand how the mind
sees these first principles enter its field of vision. I mean
the first principles of speculative reason, the principles
of identity, sufficient reason, finality, and causality. I
shall not deal with the principle of noncontradiction. For
it directly concerns logic, not metaphysics, and is but the
logical form of the principle of identity. It is the latter
reflected onto the plane of the life lived by objects in the
mind as objects of knowledge, the principle of identity
applied to logical affirmation and negation.

The Principle of Identity

2. No sooner do we possess the intuition of intelligible
extra-mental being than it divides, so to speak under our
eyes, into two conceptual objects. On the one side there
is being as simply existing or capable of existence, as
simply given to the mind, or, if you prefer, as a "thing"
in the modern sense of the word. For the ancients thing
was synonymous with essence. To the moderns, it would

seem it primarily signifies a simple existent actually given. On one side, then, there is being given *to* the mind. On the other side, in another concept which is still being, but under a different aspect, being is perceived as involving certain exigencies and certain laws, or, if you prefer, as recognized, admitted, affirmed *by* the mind—or as perfection and determination. These two complementary aspects of being are apprehended by the mind, distinguished, in a purely ideal fashion, as two different concepts expressed by the same word. Their difference, which we may term *functional,* is revealed simply in the use which the mind makes of the concept or notion of being, in the latter case as subject, in the former as predicate.

Then the mind intuits that in these two functionally different notions it is thinking of *the same thing.* It sees intuitively the first principle of all which it will formulate thus: *each being is what it is.* Here *"each being"* is being given to the mind and *"what it is"* is its intelligible determination, being as affirmed by the mind. Being thus, if we may say so, duplicates itself. To its aspect as posited in existence it adds its aspect as intelligibly determined, as an essential quality.

In his book, *Le Sens Commun et la Philosophie de l'être,* Père Garrigou-Lagrange suggests another formula which amounts to the same thing: *Every being is of a determinate nature which constitutes it what it is.* In his explanation of this formula, however, he seems to admit that in the statement of the principle of identity there is a transition from being itself, *ens,* to the first of the transcendentals which he recognizes with the scholastics, namely *res.* Being, he seems to hold, is understood as *ens* in the subject, as *res* in the predicate. I am not sure that this explanation is correct. I do not think that we pass in this way from one transcendental to another. I hold, rather, that we are concerned with the same transcendental *ens* envisaged under two different aspects, in one case *ens ut existens,* being as existing actually or possibly, *seu positum extra nihil* or posited outside nothingness, in the other with *ens ut quid essentiale, seu ponens in re,* being as something essential or as positing in an object, as signifying in it a particular intelligible perfection, a particular essential determination.

Obviously I am disputing with Père Lagrange a trifling point of terminology. For when he speaks in this connection of the transcendental *res* it is precisely inasmuch as *res* signifies the essential. Whatever may be the subtle distinction in our ways of explaining the point, the two formulas are equivalent statements of the same primary intuition, my formula "Every being is what it is" and Père Lagrange's "Every being is of a determinate nature."

3. But there are other ways, perhaps more significant, of stating this same principle of identity. Dr. Gerald Phelan prefers to say *being is being,* and in my opinion there is very much to be said for his preference. Properly explained this formula is seen to be extremely comprehensive. *Being is being,* this means first of all, "Each thing is what it is," the very formula I first suggested. But it also means, and in this case the predication and affirmation concern the act of existence, "What exists exists." This is no tautology, it implies an entire metaphysic. What is posited outside its causes exercises an activity, an energy which is existence itself. To exist is to *maintain oneself and to be maintained* outside nothingness; *esse* is an act, a perfection, indeed the final perfection, a splendid flower in which objects affirm themselves. Moreover, the formula also means "Being is not nonbeing." And this also, far from being tautologous, is pregnant with meaning. Being is being, it is not so simple as you might suppose, it is being, it possesses resources and mysteries. The principle of identity affirms the affluence, the luxury of being.

What an excellent thing it is that we are compelled to stammer, debate, and dispute, that we meet with technical difficulties in formulating the first self-evident intellectual principle. It is indeed proof that it is not a matter of formulas but a living intuition whose purely spiritual light incomparably transcends all the words in the dictionary.

The principle of identity is concerned with being outside the mind, with the implications of being at least possible, and is thus not a law of thought but the first law of objects outside the mind apprehended in the intuition of being. Even in this case St. Thomas's most important dictum concerning the judgment is still verified. For there is a conceptual difference between the subject and the predicate. The principle of identity is not tautologous. For there is in it a conceptual difference between the subject and predicate. They do not, functionally at least, present to the mind the same formal object, even though in both cases the same term being is employed. And it is the distinctive characteristic of the judgment to recognize the identity in the concrete object of what thus differs conceptually. In this case this identity is recognized by a simple inspection of the terms.

4. Observe that in current speech seeming tautologies often prove most significant propositions. When we say, *What is done is done,* or when Pilate said, *What I have written I have written,* the words have an appallingly definite meaning.

If we now transfer this implication of the principle of identity to the summit of being, to God, we are confronted with a formula which with the same words, the same exterior and material expressions, conveys meanings poles asunder. This is a fact which must interest the philosopher extremely. On the one hand there is the formula of the Koran, on the other the same formula as Christians understand it: "God is God." It is the principle of identity itself applied to the Divine Essence, the *Divine Being.* It is most interesting to notice how this single formula can express two conceptions, two intellectual views diametrically opposed.

The formula of the Mahometan "God is God," means that God is so rigorously one and incommunicable as necessarily to render impossible the mysteries of the Trinity and the Incarnation. It has thus an exclusive and negative significance. From the philosophic standpoint, the essential error here is to apply the principle of identity to God as it is applied to a creature, delimiting Him and confining Him within Himself as though to be Himself limited and confined Him. Thus He is immured, a God immured in a transcendence of death. In short, the superabundance of the Divine Being is denied, a superabundance which must be infinite as that Being itself, if from the outset, from its first intuition, being has been in fact perceived as superabounding. Islam denies this superabundance of the Divine Being which, as revelation alone can inform us, is manifested in God by the plurality of Persons and also, as unaided reason would have sufficed to disclose, by the fact that God is Love, a truth which is also denied by Mahometan orthodoxy. For Mahometans consider that to say God is Love is to ascribe a passion to Him. That is why the mystic Al Hallaj was crucified by the doctors of the Koran.

That God is loving, that He is Love itself is, as I have just said, a truth which unaided reason could have discovered, the highest truth it could have attained by its own powers. But in fact it did not attain it. The aid of revelation was necessary. If the revelation made to Moses of the Divine Name, "I am that I am," taught reason from above what it could have, but had not in fact, discovered, this is far truer of the revelation made to St. John "God is Love." Note, however: in view of the relationship in which creatures stand to God, the affirmation that God should not only be loved but that He loves, I mean with the distinctive *madness* of love, and that there can be relations of friendship, mutual self-giving, community of life, and the sharing of a common bliss between God and His creatures, implies the supernatural order of grace and charity. And it is this supernatural truth and this experience which lead the reason on to understand what is meant by the statement that God is Love, insofar as it enunciates a revealed truth of the natural order, which concerns God regarded in Himself, even though no creature existed. As I said in my last lecture, the most resplendent manifestation of the Divine glory within the scope of our reason is that the love which presupposes understanding and is above all a superflux, an ultimate superabundance of the life of spirits, is in God identical with His essence and His existence. In this sense Love is His Name par excellence —it is His gospel Name.

Thus the same formula, couched in the same words, God is God, when it is understood in the Christian sense has a totally different meaning to that which it possesses in the Koran. It signifies the infinite superabundance of the Divine Being, the transcendence of a glorious and exultant Deity, a transcendent life. That God is God means, what reason can know, that His being is not only being and not only knowledge but also love. It also means, and this we can know only by revelation, that He is indeed One and Incommunicable, but with a generosity which is of His very essence and which requires within Himself the Trinity of Persons and renders the Incarnation possible. God is a Trinity of Persons, such is His intimate life, and He is so accessible to human nature that He can be the Person in whom the nature of a man subsists.

If we grasp the fact that the principle of identity is not simply the material repetition of the same logical term but expresses the extramental coherence and overflowing wealth of being in all its analogous degrees, we shall understand that this axiom has its supreme exemplification in God Himself, in the first Principle of being, who is Truth and Love, and in the Trinity of Persons which is known only by revelation, and escapes the grasp of the philosopher's reason abandoned to its own powers.

II. The Principle of Sufficient Reason

5. Here also we observe that being divides itself, so to speak, into two objects of thought, two conceptual objects, which, however, are throughout being itself. In this instance, however, the operation is of a totally different nature to what it was in the case of the principle of

identity. On the one hand, there is being taken simply as what exists or can exist, the transcendental *ens,* and on the other hand there is being as transcendentally true. We pass over to the transcendental *truth,* to being as it confronts the intellect. And the latter word is taken in the most general and most indeterminate sense, no distinction being yet made between created intellect and the Uncreated. Being here confronts us as satisfying the natural desire, fulfilling the essential aim of the intellect. It must do this because it is its end, because the intellect is made for being.

We can say, therefore—I am trying to express the original intuition formulated by the principle of sufficient reason—that *being must be the sufficient good of intellect.* And this guides us directly to God, the Being *that is of itself the perfectly sufficient good of intellect,* the Being that is fully self-sufficient in the intelligible order, and constitutes the beatitude both of His own and of every intellect. But in fact we are confronted not with God beheld intuitively but with a host of other beings which are deficient. Therefore we cannot enunciate our intellectual perception of the bond between *ens* and *verum* without introducing a distinction. We must say: *being must either possess its intelligible sufficiency of itself, a se, or derive it from some other being, ab alio.* This is a preliminary and approximate statement of the principle of sufficient reason.

In other words, the intellect which is made for being inasmuch as it is intelligible must possess it complete and fully determined. It is not satisfied with regarding the being of an object as a simple fact, by the mere fact that an object exists. It will find rest and satisfaction only in what completes and determines the object inasmuch as it is intelligible, inasmuch as it confronts a faculty of knowledge. Since, however, intelligibility goes hand in hand with being, that which determines an object in respect of intelligibility is that which grounds it in respect of being, grounds its being, in other words *that in virtue of which it is.* We have thus brought out the notion of sufficient reason. It is that in virtue of which an object is. We must, therefore, enunciate the principle of sufficient reason in one of the two following ways: *Everything which is, to the extent to which it is, possesses a sufficient reason for its being;* that is to say, is grounded in being, so that, to put it in another way, it is capable of explaining itself to the intellect, though not necessarily to *our* intellect; *whatever is, is intelligibly determined; whatever is, has that whereby it is.* Both these formulas must be taken in the most general sense. .

6. This principle has a far more general scope and significance than the principle of causality. For the principle of sufficient reason is exemplified in cases in which the efficient cause plays no part. For instance, man's rationality is the ground, the sufficient reason of his *risibilitas* and *docilitas.* Similarly the essence of the triangle is the ground of its properties, and there is no difference of being, no real distinction between the properties of the triangle and its essence. Again God's essence is the ground of His existence, He exists *a se,* He is Himself the sufficient reason of His *esse,* the ground of His existence, since His essence is precisely to exist. ` `

This expression *a se* itself possesses a transcendent meaning, which, moreover, presupposes the entire analogy of being. It has often been misconceived by philosophers, by Descartes in particular. Descartes, understanding the Divine aseity univocally, thought himself compelled to choose between an exclusively logical and purely negative conception of this aseity as meaning simply that God *has no* cause, and an ontological and positive conception as meaning that God is *the cause of Himself,* in virtue of the infinite fullness of His essence. Not only did Descartes confuse sufficient reason with efficient cause, he conceived the Divine existence univocally. He reduced it, like the existence of creatures, to the mere fact of being posited outside nothingness, *natural* or entitative existence. Its Divinity can then consist only in the fact that it implies a perfect and an infinite efficacy. It is an earthbound philosophy. The Divine existence is infinitely more than this. It is an act of intellection, an existence of *knowledge* or *intellection*. That is why to affirm that God exists is not simply to state an empirical fact, to affirm an existence, even a necessary existence. It is to affirm an intelligible justification of existence which is eternal, an eternal and infinite satisfaction of an infinite demand for intelligibility, an infinitely full repose for the intellect.

A se: the Divine aseity does not signify a simple necessity, like geometrical necessity. The expression relates to the principle of sufficient reason, itself based on the intelligibility of being. It signifies that God's being *fully satisfies the intellect.* If the philosopher could place himself at God's standpoint while retaining his human way of conceiving, since God exists by His essence and His essence is His very act of knowing, he would say: God is in virtue of Himself, because He is intellection, He exists because He knows Himself and His truth, because He is the infinite fullness of intelligibility in pure act thinking Itself, because His existence, His nature, is the eternally subsistent act of understanding. Moreover, in knowing He wills Himself, loves Himself, and this also is His existence, an existence of love. There is a superabundance of intelligibility in the Divine Being which can thus be the infinitely sufficient reason of Its own existence.

7. At a later stage we can reduce, or rather logically attach, the principle of sufficient reason to the principle of identity, by a *reductio ad absurdum.* This is a reflex operation which may, for example, be described compendiously as follows. The expression *in virtue of which,* when we say that in virtue of which an object is, must have a meaning or be meaningless. If it is meaningless philosophy is futile, for philosophers look for a sufficient ground of things. If, on the other hand, it has a meaning, it is evident that in virtue of the principle of noncontradiction it is identical with the meaning of the phrase *that without which* an object is not. If, therefore, anything exists which has no sufficient reason for its existence, that is to say which has neither in itself nor in something else, ﹚

that in virtue of which it is, this object exists and does not exist at the same time. It does not exist because it lacks that without which it does not exist. This *reductio ad absurdum* proves that to deny the principle of sufficient reason is to deny the principle of identity. But the proof is a product of reflection. The original manifestation, spontaneous and intuitive, of the principle of sufficient reason, is as I have described it above. Being is too rich to be given to us solely in the concept of being. It divides into two objects of thought conceptually different whose real identity we perceive immediately, namely being itself and an object of thought "grounded in existence" or intelligibly determined or "apt (in virtue of itself or of something else) to perfect the movement of intelligence."

Now observe that this intelligibility which accompanies being is in pure act only in the Divine Being. Not only is it the prerogative of God to be intellection in pure act, an act of knowledge in pure act, it is also His prerogative, indeed it is the same thing, to be intelligibility in pure act. You will therefore see at once that any philosophy which claims that all things should be perfectly transparent to the intellect, contain nothing whatever that baffles comprehension, must not be in the slightest degree opaque, any such system of absolute intellectualism is inevitably pantheistic. For it ascribes to creatures this intelligibility in pure act. If things are not God they must comprise a certain measure of unintelligibility inasmuch as they originate from nothingness. If in truth intelligibility accompanies being, it is obvious that insofar as anything is affected with nonentity it must possess a root of unintelligibility. Its relative nonentity is also a relative unintelligibility. We can now understand why the doctrine of *dunamis, potentia,* is of such great metaphysical importance. At one extreme are the systems of absolute intellectualism, Spinozism for example. At the other are philosophies of absolute irrationalism, for example that of Schopenhauer. Between these contrasted errors there rises like a peak such a system as Aristotle's, which perceives that being and intelligibility go hand in hand, and that in consequence of this all beings other than God must comprise in their metaphysical structure together with a factor of relative nonentity a factor of relative unintelligibility.

To this potentiality in all creatures and therefore in all created goods corresponds the dominating indifference of the will. The will is specified by good as such, that is to say it is unable as soon as it comes into operation to will anything without first tending to a good chosen as absolute. It thus of its own fiat renders efficacious the particular good which the understanding presents to it, and which determines it. For it pours out upon that particular good, of itself wholly incapable of determining it, the superabundant determination it receives from its necessary object, good as such. It gratuitously makes that good purely and simply good for itself—the subject—in virtue, to put it so, of the fullness of intelligible determination with which it overflows. Thus the principle of sufficient reason plays no more magnificent part than its part in making possible the freedom of the will.

A further remark. This principle of sufficient reason is universal though its application is analogous. It is not valid only for this or that kind of being, for created or contingent being, for example, but for all being without exception. I have just shown that it is as valid for God as for creatures, though in a totally different fashion. The principle of sufficient reason precedes the division of being into potency and act. To apprehend its necessity there is no need first to have recognized this distinction.

8. Finally we may note that the principle of sufficient reason is necessary in virtue of what the school of St. Thomas and Aristotle call the second mode of *perseitas,* perseity. On this point I refer you to the Second Analytics Book I, Ch. 3, tenth lecture by St. Thomas.

In short, Thomists distinguish two ways in which a predicate can be attributed necessarily or per se to a subject, therefore two modes of necessary attribution. In the first of these the notion of the predicate is implied in that of the subject. This is the only mode taken into consideration by the moderns when they discuss self-evident principles. And it certainly applies to the principle of identity. But for the scholastics there is a second mode of perseity. In this the predicate is not implicit in the notion of the subject, as belonging to its definition. On the contrary, it is the subject which is implied by the predicate, not as part of its definition but as being *the distinctive subject* of that predicate, as for example *nose* of *snub*.

St. Thomas, replying by anticipation to Kant's criticism of the principle of causality, observes that this principle is necessary in virtue of the second mode of perseity.[1] Let us suppose a caused object. The relation to a cause does not enter into the definition of its being. Scrutinize as you will the notion of being, of contingent being or being which comes into existence, you will not discover that it is necessarily caused. You will not find the predicate in the notion of the subject. It is in the notion of the predicate "caused" that you will discover its demand for the subject, contingent being. *Hujusmodi ens (sc. per participationem, seu non per se) non potest esse, quin sit causatum; sicut nec homo quin sit risibilis.* An object of this kind, i.e. one that exists by participation, not by itself, cannot but be caused, just as there cannot be a man who is not risible. St. Thomas takes for his example the faculty of laughter in man. The power to laugh is a *passio propria,* a distinctive passion whose subject is *man.* And what he says of the principle of causality is true of the principle of sufficient reason. In the same way, if you consider the notion *even or odd,* their distinctive subject is whole number. You therefore say, "Whole numbers are even or odd." In like manner, if you consider the notion "grounded in existence," "having a sufficient reason," the distinctive subject of such a notion is being. You therefore enunciate the principle of sufficient reason. Being is grounded in being. "Everything which is, insofar as it is, has a sufficient reason for being." The principle is *per se secundo modo.*

[1] *Sum. Theol.* I, 44, ad. I.

III. The Principle of Finality: First Aspect

9. I have just said that the principle of sufficient reason precedes the division of being into potency and act. I have now to point out that the principle of finality covers these two planes of potency and act. For there are two quite different expressions of this one principle. Among the scholastics the following formula is very common. Potency essentially refers to act, *potentia dicitur ad actum*. Here potency is regarded as passive potency or potentiality in its reference to the act which determines and perfects it. But there is another and a more important statement of the same principle: Every agent acts in view of an end, *omne agens agit propter finem*. These are two quite different statements of the same principle. The former holds sway throughout the entire lower order of potency. It tells us that all potency is referred to the act which determines it. The latter, on the contrary, is concerned with the order of activity, of actuality and perfection. And since of its nature act precedes potency, this latter statement is the principal one.

10. We will now consider this principle of finality. Being, always in virtue of that wealth of which I have spoken, divides in a third way, altogether unlike the two former. We will first contemplate objects from below, from the standpoint of the potentiality implied by becoming. On the one hand being, taken in its lowest degree, is objectified as simply potential, as a capacity of being determined, as *potency*. On the other hand this same being or rather possibility of being is objectified as *referred to act*. So we affirm: potency is referred to act. Fundamentally it is the very notion of potency which is thus explained. For of its notion potency, and this is its intelligibility itself, all the intelligibility it possesses, is

reference to a particular act. We can conceive potency only in reference to an act. Pure indeterminancy is unthinkable. Therefore potency and reference to an act are synonymous. Here we are concerned with the first mode of perseity.

In view of what was said above of the dynamism of being, the fact that every being follows a tendency, an inclination, I affirm that potency has a natural desire, a natural appetite for act. This reference of potency to act is an ontological desire, a desire for act, potency itself.

11. We could quite well adopt this standpoint of potency and its transcendental reference to act if we would discuss finality. This is Roland Dalbiez's procedure in his study of the principle of finality.[2] He begins with the fact of movement. He then observes that reason compels us to distinguish in movement two factors, the new determination acquired, and its subject. "Plato had already proved as against the followers of Heraclitus that the notion of a movement without a subject, a movement which should not be the movement of something, a movement which should be nothing but movement, is simply unthinkable. We are therefore obliged to admit beneath the new determinations a real indeterminacy. Behind the act we posit potency. . . ."

This concept of potency "is essentially relative. If we attempt to detach it from its reference to act it vanishes." And he concludes: "This foreordination of potency to act is finality. The precise meaning of finality is now clear. It is the reference of potency to act. . . . We cannot conceive that anything you please *is* anything else you please. And when we perceive that action is a mode of being, we see that it is equally unthinkable that anything you please *produces* just anything you please. But . . . action takes place in time. It follows therefore anything you please *cannot* produce just anything you please.

[2] *Premier Cahier de Philosophie de la Nature,* devoted to transformism, last chapter, Paris, Vrin, 1927.

Determination brings us to ordination and ordination to foreordination."

As the same writer justly observes, the problem of finality must be stated in terms of the simple and the element, not in terms of an ordered complex or plurality of elements reduced to the unity of a given order. This is a secondary consideration. The root of the matter, on the contrary, is the relation of the subject of change to the determination which actualizes it, the relation of a potency to its act. It is this which imposes upon the mind the notion of finality.

Throughout his study Dalbiez does not move from his standpoint, the reference of potency to act. Even when he speaks of the cause or active potency which produces an effect he still considers it as passing from potency to act. This, be it observed incidentally, is the reason why the same word potency can be used to signify two very different things, both the potentiality—the passive potency referred to an act which determines it—and the active potency, for example the "powers" (potencies) or energies of the soul. We call the intelligence or the will a power. Why the same word? [3] Because throughout the order of created being even active faculties, even active potencies or powers comprise a potential factor. When they act, and actively produce the perfection which is their act, they perfect themselves, they become more perfect. Therefore they pass themselves from potency to act. A created agent becomes, it acquires a final perfection by producing its effect. For reason these are two different things: to produce an effect that is to perfect something else, if the action is transitive, one's self if it is immanent and oneself to become, to pass to a final perfection. But these two things are combined in the action of every created agent. The tree acquires a final perfection, passes itself from a lesser to a greater perfection by producing its fruit. In the same way when hy-

[3] In Latin and French the same word *potentic, puissance,* is used for potency and for power. Tr.

drogen and oxygen, by combining, give birth to water, there is a passage to a greater ontological perfection, not indeed as regards the hydrogen and oxygen themselves, which no longer exist, but as regards the prime matter which is the common subject of the change. Therefore from my present standpoint I maintain that an agent, an active cause, cannot produce just any effect you please, precisely because it cannot become just anything you please, cannot acquire any and every final perfection. We therefore remain throughout at the standpoint of potency referred to the act which perfects and determines it.

12. Nevertheless there is a second aspect of causal activity to be considered, not as hitherto that of potency but that of activity itself which as such, when taken purely in its character as activity, does not necessarily and of itself involve potency, though in creatures it does, in fact, involve it. That is why power, active power or potency, can in this second sense be ascribed to God and that we call Him omnipotent. In this case the agent is considered *precisely as active*. Things are viewed from above, under the aspect of what even in becoming, though not in becoming alone, is actuality and perfection. I thus come to analyze the second statement of the principle of finality, not *potentia dicitur ad actum* but the supreme, most metaphysical and most profound statement of the principle, namely *omne agens agit propter finem*. Here also we shall discover once more the same division of being into two conceptual objects presented to the mind by different notions and identified in a judgment.

SIXTH LECTURE

The Principle of Finality (Second Aspect)

The Most Profound and Most Universal Statement of the Principle of Finality

1. In the last lecture we have studied the first statement of the principle of finality, adopting the standpoint of potential being. We saw that it is of the very essence of potency to be referred to act and to be knowable only through the act to which it is referred. *Potentia dicitur ad actum* is one of the two statements of the principle of finality.

If we adopt another standpoint, that of actuality itself, the standpoint of the perfection which every action involves, of the communication of being and act, we attain a more profound and a more universal view of the principle of finality, and a more instructive view. It is expressed by the classical Thomist statement of the principle: *Omne agens agit propter finem,* every agent acts in view of an end. It is this second aspect of the principle of finality that I wish to consider today. We shall be brought back to the burden of these reflections

107

on the first principles. As is the case with every principle intuitively apprehended by the intellect, being so to speak divides in face of the mind into two distinct conceptual objects which are nevertheless being itself, and which the judgment identifies "a priori," that is to say, because these concepts compel the identification.

What in the present instance are these two distinct conceptual objects? Being is here apprehended under the aspect of action or operation, that is to say as positing a terminal act, *actus secundus,* in which an essence is perfected and fructifies, an act over and above the simple fact of existing, the terminal act of existence. On the one hand being will be considered as *Agent,* on the other hand as tendency to a *Good* to which the agent is referred as such—in other words an *End.* We shall analyze these two notions.

Agent and End

2. What is the content of this notion, agent? I am employing the term "agent" which is far more universal than the term "efficient cause" of which I shall speak later. The term agent is as general as the term action.

As you know, the scholastics distinguish two sorts of action essentially different, so that the notion and the term action are simply analogous as applied to both. They are transitive and immanent action. Immanent action consists not in doing or producing anything but in perfecting the agent's being, that is in the case of the most purely immanent, namely spiritual, actions. For it consists in a terminal act, *an Operation,* which is itself an *Existence* of an absolutely (super-subjective) superior order, for example an act of intellection or will. For the Thomist such an immanent action does not belong to the predicament "action" in Aristotle's list of predicaments. Since it is a pure inner perfection of the subject it belongs to the category of quality.

Now the term agent possesses the same analogical comprehensiveness as the term action and can relate either to the agent capable of transitive action or to the agent capable of immanent action. That is why I prefer the term agent to the term efficient cause which is restricted to a transitive action, or at most extends to whatever in immanent activity may be concomitantly or virtually productive and transitive.

This notion of agent involves in the first place the actuality of a being in act possessing a particular determination and perfection which constitute it what it is. It also implies that this being communicates an actuality, a perfection, either to another in the case of transitive action, or to itself in the case of immanent. As I said just now, we are here concerned with the order of operation, which is an *actus secundus,* that is a terminal act, distinct, except in God, from simple existence, which is also a terminal act, a certain perfection, a certain term. As God is His existence, so is He His action. And His action is His existence. He is therefore in His absolute simplicity the final act alike in the order of existence and in the order of operation. As I have already said, His existence is His understanding and His love without even a virtual distinction from either.

The terminal act in the order of operation, the operative terminal act, with which I am now dealing, is first found, very imperfectly, in transitive action. Here there is a communication of actuality in the order of what the ancients called entitative natural being: one body modifies another entitatively. It is most perfect in the case of immanent action. On the lowest level of immanent action, the living organism constructs and perfects itself entitatively. It becomes increasingly perfect as we advance in the scale of immanent actions. In operations above the vegetative level there is a communication of actuality in the order no longer of entitative but of intentional being, the being, that is to say, in virtue of which a being is more than itself, exists over and above its own existence. It is the intentional being of knowledge or love. It is the intentional being by which, in the case of knowledge, the knower can become something other than himself, indeed, all things. This perfects the knowing subject in himself. It is the intentional being by which, in the case of love, the subject can exist by way of gift and can overflow to all things, which thus become himself to himself. And this will be completed by another sort of union, the real union with the object of love.

3. I shall therefore study being as agent or in the order of operation. Now we know better what this means. Another object of thought, which is still, as always, being but under another aspect, is revealed at the same time— namely being as good exercising its functions as good, being as the good or perfection which the agent desires and toward which it tends and inclines in virtue of its very being. Being as agent *is reference to and determination to* a particular good, is appetite, tendency, desire, an urge, toward a surplus, a superabundance, a glory. And this reference is the very ground of the agent's operation, the reason why that operation is posited in existence.

This then is the second of the two aspects, "inspects," into which being divides from this point of view, and which are identified in reality. And it is the principle of finality in its primary metaphysical significance. *Being is love of good, every being is the love of a good*, and this love is the very ground of its action.

We may observe, by the way, that operation is a surplus, a *plus* in respect of the agent. But where shall we find its sufficient reason save in the agent from which it proceeds? Plus, however, cannot proceed from minus. Hence the agent must be itself in some way a reference, a tendency to the action in question, a love of it. To the extent to which it is a pure agent, its action manifests the fullness of the agent's actuality, of its being as tendency and love. It is *actus perfecti,* the act of a perfect being. To the extent, on the other hand, to which the action, as happens with every created creature, perfects the agent, the latter is not purely an agent. It passes from potency to act, and must therefore be a "Patient" as well as an agent, be moved by something else. ˏ ˏ

I have just said that being is love of good. Every being is the love of a good which is in the first place its own action. Being as agent does not tend to this good in order to be actualized or perfected by it. This would be a return to the standpoint of potential being which we adopted in the last lecture. It tends to it, even if incidentally it acquires actuality and perfection, in order to perfect itself or something else, to impart to itself or another a perfection, a surplus. The good to which it thus tends is called an *end.* It is an end for the agent. And the love of this end is the formal reason of the agent's action.

Consider first the order of natural being, *ens entitativum,* of what may be called natural agents, that is to say agents determined to act by their nature. The being of a plant, for example, is a radical love and appetite to grow and reproduce its species, the being of fire a love and appetite to burn, of a bird to fly and sing.

Turn to the order of intentional being, of agents which in the widest sense we may term voluntary, that is to say determined to act by an inclination consequent upon knowledge. A bird, for instance, sees a grain of millet, a child a fruit. By the very fact that their look is thus informed by intention, something is produced in them according to intentional being, a mode namely of tendential existence, which is their respective desire for the seed or the fruit in virtue of which they proceed to take it. Friend loves friend. Here also an intentional being is produced in the friend who loves, a mode of intentional existence which *is* the love itself by which he tends inwardly toward his friend as toward a second self. And in virtue of this love for his friend he will act. He will will and do what is good for his friend. Thus *being as agent or in operation* (whether the agent be regarded in its entative or natural or in its intentional being, in which a particular inclination proceeds or is elicited from a voluntary agent) *is reference to an end or love of a good,* and this reference is the ground of the agent's action.

The good to which the agent is referred, the end to which it tends, is in the first place the agent's operation itself, inasmuch as it is to be posited in existence, because this is his own good. And it is from this standpoint that we must primarily envisage, as I have just done, the principle of finality. The proximate end in view of which an agent acts is its action itself. But ends are obviously subordinated one to another as grounds of action. From the proximate end to the end next in order, from good to good we must ascend, if we would account for the action of the most insignificant agent, to the *absolute good* which is the universal End, and which gives rise to all the rest, to every communicable good, to all ends and tendencies.

Analytic Discussion

4. We will now reflect upon the conclusions just established. We shall catch sight of doctrinal backgrounds, of metaphysical truths which indeed come into view *after* the intuition of the principle of finality but which will enable us to grasp better its meaning and bearing. I continue then to consider being as agent. Only God's Being consists of self-knowledge and self-love. It is not so with any creature. God has no intentional being. For by His very essence He is eminently all things, since His essence is His Intellection and His Love themselves. Hence His entitative Being does not require completion by an intentional Being, It is fulfilled by the *actus purus* which is Himself. In every being but God, action, whether transitive or immanent, is distinct from the agent. To be a Euclidean triangle is the same thing as to have the sum of the angles equal to two right angles. Here there is no real distinction between the property and the essence. There is merely a conceptual distinction, one of the terms being the ground of the other. But to be a man who thinks is

not the same thing as the action of thinking, just as the action of burning differs from fire. If we take account of this real distinction between action and agent it will be evident that, if the agent performs a particular action, produces a certain effect, there must be a sufficient reason for it, that is to say before the action is performed it is determined that the agent shall produce this particular effect, perform this particular action rather than any other. As we have seen, for it is indeed the principle of finality, the agent has a determination, which is an appetite or a love, it has a determination, a reference to a particular good by which it perfects itself or something else, and which is its action.

Now, however, I wish to consider this relation of the agent to its action, an action distinct from itself. The bird is determined to fly by its essence or nature as a bird. It has a relation, a determination to that action, and this determination is its very essence. Similarly, hydrogen and oxygen are determined to produce water in combination by their nature as hydrogen and oxygen. They have a relation which is their very essence to the generation of this new body. To be determined to a term presupposes an ordination, a relation to that term. In the case of being as agent, this ordination or determination—which is an appetite and a love and which is identical with the being itself, entitative or intentional—must exist between the agent and the term or the action *before* the agent acts and produces its effect. This is evident. For the determination is the ground of the agent's action, and the ground of the action must precede, at least with a priority of nature, the action itself. In the case of natural agents this determination or reference to the action is identical with the agent's essence, the first principle of its operations. To be fire, is, as I have just said, to be ordained by that very fact to the action of burning, to be a bird is to be ordained to the action of flying.

I will pursue this train of thought. How can there be a relation, an ordination between two things which do not exist in any fashion, or between a thing which exists and a thing which does not? For a relation or ordination to exist between two terms both terms must exist. Therefore an effect or an action must somehow exist if the agent is to be determined, ordained, or inclined toward it. What does this mean? It means that the action or effect must exist before it is produced or realized.

5. But how in the name of heaven is this possible? Only if the action or effect exists *as present in thought,* with the existence of knowledge. Only in this way can it exist —in thought, in knowledge—before it exists in reality. All this follows of necessity from our previous considerations. But where will it take us? We have seen that in the case of natural agents the determination to the effect or the action is the agent's essence. Now we are compelled to admit that before being posited in their natural existence, the agent's action and therefore his essence alike exist with an existence superior to their merely natural existence, an existence of knowledge or thought.

We may know nothing of this knowledge and thought. We do not necessarily know whether it is pure act or not, whether it is transcendent of things or immanent in them. Nor have we at this first moment, when the self-evident principles disclose themselves to us, yet established the metaphysical conclusions about God's nature. But we do at least know implicitly, as soon as we have stated the principle of finality, that natural existence depends upon an existence of knowledge, that the action of objects would be unintelligible if they did not depend upon a thought, therefore that at the beginning, at the root of things, in a fashion which as yet we cannot clearly determine, there is thought. The agent's essence and its action must be present in a thought on which that essence depends and which conceives it as an ordination or determination to that action, an ontological inclination to the action, an ontological love of it. *The dynamism of being presupposes knowledge and thought, the forming Word.* We see, then, that at the original formation of things, as it were their metaphysical womb, there is something analogous to what we call intellect, though at the outset we cannot determine its nature more accurately. Hence it is enough to posit the object I term fire for the action of burning to follow of itself, under the requisite conditions. But to posit this thing I term fire is precisely to posit a reference, preordination, or radical determination to the action of burning, an action conceived by a thought as that which this particular object is to produce and perform.

We see, therefore, that the sufficient reason of an agent's action, that which determines it to a particular action or effect rather than any other is the effect, the action, itself—not as produced and accomplished, but as that which is to be produced, accomplished, and therefore as preconceived by a thought, so as to preordain the agent to that action. This, then, is what completes the notion of the final cause and renders it clear: the effect itself as foreknown and determining the agent that tends to it by a radical love, or by an elicited love.

6. You see that we can most truly say that the bird flies because it possesses wings, because it is a bird. But what then is it to be a bird? It is to be determined to fly. This precisely is the foundation of the principle of finality. It is its primary and principal aspect. The arrow is determined to its target and set in motion by the archer. An accidental determination of this kind, however, is but a secondary example of the principle which it illustrates, and obviously takes a second place. The reference to the goal possessed by the arrow is imparted to it from without by the archer, is accidental to its nature. If, then, we begin our study of the principle of finality with the aid of such instances of it, we expose ourselves to the charge of having generalized and transferred to natural agents what is true only of the actions of intelligent agents, to the suspicion of anthropomorphism. If, on the other hand, we begin with natural agents, we see that the very nature of things must be conceived as a radical determination to an action or effect. If we forget every example taken from the behavior of man, of a reasonable being, and look at things simply from the point of view of being as agent, we recognize that the notion of finality, which forces itself

upon us more powerfully than ever, does not involve even the shadow of anthropomorphism.

If after these examples of actions belonging to the entitative order we rise in the hierarchy of operations, we arrive at a determination to act which, instead of being, as hitherto, identical with the agent's being, proceeds from his knowledge and his elicited inclination, from his intelligence and will.

Here also we observe that the action differs from the agent. The action of an intelligent being endowed with will is other than himself. But in this case the determination to action, the transcendental reference to it, is no longer the agent's nature. Nor yet is it a mere accident which modifies the agent's natural being, as was the case with the arrow externally determined to its target. The determination to action now belongs to the intentional being. It arises from a tendency, an inclination, which follows knowledge.

When finally we rise to God, the First of all beings, action no longer differs from the agent. It is the Agent Himself. But the reference to it, that is to the very essence of the Agent, is nevertheless intellectual and voluntary, as in the preceding case is God's love of the Divine essence and goodness. God necessarily wills and loves the good which is His being, and this love, because it is without even a virtual distinction from it, is itself His essence, and His existence Itself. To be as love, to exist as a gift, a breath, a super-subjective super-effluence is, like the super-subjective super-existence of His knowledge, not intentional in God, but His natural existence itself. A new aspect of the Divine aseity is thus disclosed to us. I said in my last lecture that if the philosopher could adopt God's point of view while retaining his human fashion of forming concepts, the affirmation that "the Pure Act" exists *a se* would mean God exists because He knows Himself, that is to say God is because His essence is to know Himself. Now I say that God is of Himself also means that He is because He loves Himself, He exists because His existence is to love Himself. ·

And in this very act of God's love for God all things

other than Himself are freely willed and loved, so that God is necessarily the end of His love and acts for an end which is His goodness and its communication. Since it is with the same act of love by which He necessarily loves His own goodness and which is His existence that He freely loves and wills creatures, He cannot love them save in reference to this goodness. He does not first will man, then the physical world for man's sake. Nor does He first will the acts of seeing, being aware, or moving, and then the animal for their sake. Nor does He first will His goodness and its communication, then creatures for its sake. He wills that the physical world *should exist* for man, that the animal should exist for the acts of seeing, being aware, and the like. And He wills that creatures should exist for His goodness and its communication. *Vult ergo hoc esse propter hoc; sed non propter hoc vult hoc.* He wills the former should exist for the sake of the latter, but not for the sake of the latter does He will the former.[1]

Thus, like the principle of sufficient reason, the principle of finality embraces being in its entirety, both uncreated as well as created being.

Supplementary Observations

7. Like the other first principles, the principle of finality can be verified analytically by a *reductio ad absurdum.* In this case the verification proceeds by attaching the principle of finality to that of identity by the intermediary of the principle of sufficient reason. This procedure is followed by all philosophers who defend finality. The elements of such a *reductio ad absurdum* were indicated in the discussion just concluded. If the agent is not predetermined to an end, its action has no sufficient reason. Thus the principle of sufficient reason is denied, and con-

[1] *Sum. Theol.* I, 19, 5.

sequently the principle of identity. But in fact the mind has thus engaged in a reflex proof. The primary view, the view which corresponds to the spontaneous intuition which constitutes the act of understanding, is, as we have seen in the first part of this lecture, the fact that in the principle of finality being is manifest under the aspect of transcendental good confronting an appetite, an inclination or love, whether that appetite is "elicited," or radical (in which case it is identical with very nature of the substance or faculty) an appetite, moreover, which is proper to being as agent. Being, too rich to express itself by the concept of being alone, divides on the one hand into the *agent,* that is being itself as able to overflow in act and in goodness, to communicate act or good, on the other hand into the *good* to which the agent is referred and determined either by its will or by its nature, as its love is voluntary or natural: and, I mean, precisely as an agent, not therefore, from this point of view, as acting to receive a perfection but either to perfect actively something else or to let its own perfection overflow.

In every creature these two aspects are blended. By perfecting something else the natural agent attains its own perfection. By knowing and loving an agent capable of immanent action receives a perfection which it confers on itself by its own activity. But these two aspects must be distinguished. And in God there is only one. Finality signifies this dynamic aspect of being, to which I called your attention in a previous lecture. *Ad omnem formam sequitur inclinatio, omne esse sequitur appetitus.* An inclination follows every form, an appetite every being. Here we are dealing with a tendency or inclination of the agent itself as such, which follows upon being as act or form, the inclination of being to superabound and to perfect, to communicate a surplus—a determinate surplus, a determinate excess of being, without which it could communicate nothing. God needs nothing. In Him there is simply this generosity and superabundance without the least connotation of receptivity or potency. His Being is love.

If He refers all things to Himself, it is not for His own good. For He has no need of them. It is for their good and for their own ontological rectitude, without which, indeed, they could not exist. They could sooner lose their nature than their ordination to God. In God there is no shade of selfishness. *Deus suam gloriam quaerit non propter se sed propter nos.* God seeks His glory not for His own sake but for ours.[2]

8. We now understand the true sense of St. Thomas's statement, frequently repeated, of the principle of finality; *omne agens agit propter finem,* every agent acts in view of an end. You will find in St. Thomas himself, summed up in his distinctive fashion, that is with an admirable simplicity, all the points I have here attempted to make. The passage in question is in the *Summa Theologica* (I—II, 1, 2). Here it is. "Matter receives form only insofar as it is moved by an agent, for nothing reduces itself from potency to act. But the agent does not move without intending an end or as preordained to an end. *Ex intentione finis.*" The formula is wholly general and universal. "For unless the agent were determined to a particular effect it would not do one thing rather than another. If, therefore, it is to produce a determinate effect, it must be preordained to a particular thing which is its end. This preordination which in a rational nature is effected by the rational appetite we term the will, is effected in other natures by what is called the natural appetite." [3]

Moreover, this formula, that every agent acts in view of an end, is the pivot on which Père Garrigou-Lagrange's magnificent book *Le Réalisme du Principe de Finalité* turns.

---

[2] *Sum. Theol.,* II–II, 132, I, ad I.

[3] *I–II, i, 2. Materia non consequitur formam nisi secundum quod movetur ab agente: nihil enim reducit se de potentia in actum. Agens autem non move nisi ex intentione finis. Si enim agens non esset determinatum ad aliquem effectum non magis ageret hoc quam illud: ad hoc ergo quod determinatum effectum producat, necesse est quod determinetur ad aliquid certum, quod habet rationem finis. Haec autem determinatio, sicut in rationali natura fit per rationalem appetitum, qui dicitur voluntas; ita in aliis fit per inclinationem naturalem, quae dicitur appetitus naturalis.*

From all that has been said we can understand why the ancients also employed another formula of equivalent meaning: *Omnis res est propter suam operationem*, everything exists for its operation. This is what I have been pointing out. As Père Garrigou-Lagrange observes, the ancients saw a difficulty at this point. A thing is a substance, an operation is an accident. Can the substance exist for the accident? Cajetan's answer is profound. *Omnis res est propter suam operationem, scilicet propter semetipsam operantem*. Everything exists for itself in operation, for inasmuch as it is in operation, it attains its ultimate actuality.

We are now in a position to criticize certain statements of the principle of finality, which are merely approximate or actually erroneous. In his book on final causes Paul Janet proposed the following formula: "Everything is determined to an end." It is faulty in two respects. In the first place God is not determined to an end. Though as I have pointed out He is the object and the end of His love, He does not exist for an end; and His being and will no more have final than they have efficient causes. And in the second place chance events, at least in respect of the entire order of created agents, have no end. That is why they are fortuitous. Therefore to defend the principle of finality the philosopher need not be able to assign an end, for example, to the shape of clouds. The sole preordaining agent on which chance events depend is the First Cause. For the rest they depend on the mutual interference of secondary causes without any preordination in the created order. On the same ground I must criticize another suggested statement of the principle of finality: "Whatever happens, happens in view of an end." That which happens by chance is precisely what happens with no end to determine it. *Every agent* indeed *acts in view of an end*, for an end. It is because the pursuit of their respective ends by different agents gives rise to a mutual interference of these lines of causation that an event occurs which is itself fortuitous. That is why St. Thomas, speaking formally, says that chance events have no cause determining their production, because they have no unity, but are merely the coincidence of a manifold, if we may so express it. The sole unity they can possess is in thought.

9. We should further observe, as St. Thomas points out (*De Potentia,* q. 5 a. I) that since, as we have just seen, "the end is a cause, only inasmuch as it moves the agent to its operation, whether the agent be determined to it by its nature or by knowledge and will, it is not the first cause in being but only in intention. Where there is no action, there is no end, as we read in the third book of the Metaphysics." On this there are three observations to be made. The end is not first in being but only in intention, inasmuch as it signifies the agent's preordination to a particular action or effect. This purifies the principle of finality from a number of adventitious interpretations which more or less consciously confuse the end with the efficient cause. The end does not act by any entitative action or motion in the strict sense. Failure to grasp this vitiated the interpretations of the principle of finality frequently proposed by the romantic philosophy of the nineteenth century. No clear distinction was made between the final cause in the strict sense and a sort of efficient causality supposed to be exercised by the end itself.

Now for my second observation. The good acts as lovable or desirable. Its function as good is to attract love. We may therefore say that the good or end "acts" on the agent or "moves" him. This language is, however, as I have just indicated, metaphorical. What is not metaphorical is that the end, in virtue of the love it evokes, is the *ground* of the agent's action. In strictest truth it determines the latter, and exercises a most genuine causality over it. How does it do this? The causality is the love itself—inasmuch as it depends upon the good or end —by which the agent tends toward that good or end. This love is sometimes the agent's being itself, sometimes the "produced" or elicited love which is evoked in the agent by the mere fact that the good in question is presented to him by knowledge. I said at the outset [4] that love of the end is the formal reason of the agent's action. This means that the true causality of the end or that in virtue of which it acts is this love which it evokes by the fact that it is known.[5] In the case of "produced," or "elicit," love this is obvious. In the case of "radical," or natural, love which is identical with the agent's being itself, with the very essence of the substance or faculty, the knowledge in question must be sought not in the agent itself, but in the thought which gives the agent being, the creative Thought. There is indeed no question here of a knowledge which evokes in God a love of the end. God is not subject to the causality of an end. He is Himself the End. As such He acts on all things, as supremely loved by them, not only as their efficient cause, and His creative knowledge orders all things to their end and good.

My third observation is this. Where there is no action, there is no final cause. Because there is no action in mathematics there is no final cause in this sphere any more than there is any efficient cause. In mathematics there is but a formal cause. This is what Aristotle meant by the very important remark on which the Thomists comment, that mathematics "are not good." Good, that is an end, has no place in mathematical explanation. You will understand from this that a philosopher such as Spinoza, who envisages the nature of metaphysics from the mathematical standpoint, must inevitably confuse the agent's relation to its action with that of the essence to its properties and thus reject finality. Finality is as impossible in Spinoza's world as in the world of mathematics.

Spinoza's God, a Deity very imperfectly immanent, is thought and extension, as we might conceive a subsistent Geometry. No more than the latter is He or can He be love. Nor can He be Himself the object and end of His love. Though we ought to love Him with an intellectual love, as we might love such a Geometry, both are

---

[4] See above p. 110.

[5] Cf. John of St. Thomas *"Quae sit causalitas finis."* Curs. Phil., Ed. Reiser, 2 pp., 276 *et sqq.*

equally incapable of returning our love or loving us first. Moreover, Spinoza's God causes things without ordaining them to any end.

We do not say that the essence of the triangle is made for its properties, which would be meaningless. Nor is this essence really distinct from its properties. This attempt to conceive the relation of the agent to its action on the model of the relation of the geometrical essence to its properties, though in fact it is impossible to eliminate completely the relation of agent to action, may help us to grasp Spinoza's conception of an immanent cause, in which there is no real distinction between the cause and that which is caused by it. Why is this? Because there is no real distinction between the essence of the triangle and its properties. Nevertheless this Spinozist cause retains the term cause and the idea of a production, an emanation. For this immanent cause, conceived on the model of the relation of the geometrical essence to its properties, retains something of the datum which it sought to reduce, namely the agent's relation to its action and effect. But in the latter case the cause is in fact distinct from the effect as it cannot be in Spinoza's immanent cause with which it is therefore incompatible. It is primarily because Spinoza failed to grasp the real distinction between the agent and its action that at the same time and with equal vehemence he denied the principle of finality and the possibility of miracles. Both alike are rejected, because you cannot deprive a triangle of its geometrical properties. If you conceive the agent's relation to its action in this geometrical fashion it becomes absurd to hold that an agent can be miraculously deprived of its operation, that the youths in the fiery furnace could fail to be burned by the fire.

10. One final observation about this principle of finality. *Omne agens agit propter finem,* every agent acts in view of an end. Like the principle of sufficient reason this is an instance of the second mode of perseity, *per se secundo modo.* When the mind perceives these two notions into which being divides beneath its eye, the notions

"Acting in view of an end" and "being that acts," it sees at once that the former involves "Being that acts" as its *subject,* not as part of its definition.

I hope the exposition I have attempted has shown you how this principle, the third of the great first principles which possess the universal range of transcendental being, imposes itself upon the intellect without the least taint of anthropomorphism. I have dealt primarily with natural agents. And on the other hand I have strictly refrained from considering the case of a manifold which concurs to produce a certain unity, in which the principle of finality is exemplified in the second degree. It was simpler to leave this out of account and confine myself to the relation or ordination of an agent to its operation, whether a natural agent, or an intelligent and voluntary agent.

In the next lecture I shall say a few words about the principle of efficient causality. I shall thus abandon the higher ground of the absolute universality possessed by the transcendentals when taken in the pure state, for the lower ground where our prospect of being is more restricted.

A species of trinity is constituted by the first principles which cover the entire field of being in all its universality, namely the principles of identity, sufficient reason, and finality. In the principle of identity we contemplate transcendental *being* itself, under two diverse aspects; in the principle of sufficient reason the mind contemplates transcendental *being* and transcendental *truth*. In the principle of finality it contemplates transcendental *being* and transcendental *good.* Below this level of absolute universality we can study contingent being. And when it contemplates contingent being, being which does not contain in itself the ground of its being, its sufficient reason, the mind catches sight of a fourth self-evident principle, the principle of efficient causality.

SEVENTH LECTURE

The Principle of Causality. Chance

I. The Principle of Causality

1. As I remarked at the close of my last lecture, to reach the principle of efficient causality we must cease to contemplate being in its entire analogical plenitude, as absolutely universal, comprising alike uncreated and created being. For the principle of causality obtains only in the latter, contingent being which is not *a se*, which does not contain in itself the entire ground of its existence.

In fact the notion of being divides before the mind into *self-existent* or absolutely necessary *being*, and this moreover before the *existence* of a self-existent being has been proved, and being which is not self-existent but *contingent*. The same division may be expressed in other terms and more technically. We may say that being divides into being in pure act and composite being, into which in one way or another a factor of potency enters. It is the second member of this division, being which contains a potential factor, being therefore which is not a *se*, that we must now study.

We are always brought back to the principle that being is richer than its objectivations, so that in the first intuitive judgments by which we apprehend it it divides into two distinct conceptual objects whose *real* identity we immediately recognize. Contingent being, being which is not self-existent, being which can be nonexistent, this conceptual object divides before our mind's eye into two objects conceptually distinct. One of these is what I propose to term "contingent being posited in existence," the other what I shall term "caused," that is to say, "having a ground, a sufficient reason other than itself." When our mind contemplates these two notions we see that in being outside the mind they are necessarily identical. Accordingly we formulate the axiom: Every contingent being has a ground other than itself, exterior to itself, that is to say an efficient cause. It is a self-evident axiom and, like the principles we have already examined, can be attached by a *reductio ad adsurdum* to the principle of identity.

For if we suppose a contingent being, a being which can be nonexistent, that is to say which does not possess its entire ground in itself, which is not self-existent, and at the same time imagine that this being which by definition does not possess its entire ground in itself has no ground outside itself, it constitutes as such a breach of the principle of sufficient reason. But a breach of the principle of sufficient reason is a breach of the principle of identity. This argument does not claim to demonstrate the principle of causality but to place those who deny it in an impasse.

2. You will observe that in all this I have not employed any spatial division, such as those which M. Le Roy's philosophy attributes to conceptual thought and in particular to the principle of causality. Nor have I generalized a psychological experience, a procedure which would have laid me open to a more or less plausible charge of anthropomorphism. I have not thought of a ball clashing with another ball, nor of a muscular effort producing a particular effect and felt by us when we exert it. On the

contrary, I have strictly adhered to the notion of ground or sufficient reason in its full abstract generality; *that in virtue of which a thing is* in the most general sense, that by which an object is determined in respect of intelligibility, that by which it can satisfy the intellect and give it rest. And it is simply this notion of sufficient reason which I have more fully determined by adding the note "other than the object of which it is the ground," a ground "exterior to the contingent being we have in view." So far, indeed, is the principle of causality from being derived from an empirical or psychological generalization that it is difficult for it to make contact with experience. I mean that when we look for concrete examples of the principle of causality every one we find proves at some point defective. Take the instance of one body striking against another. We are indeed assured by long experience that the cause of the second body's motion is, in fact, concealed here, *that* the encounter of the two bodies is the cause of that motion. But we do not perceive *in what* this cause, this sufficient reason consists. It is extremely mysterious. And for this reason our example is most unsatisfactory. Observe that one of the arguments employed by the empiricist school of philosophy, by David Hume, for example, is the assumption that the rationality and self-evidence which belong to the *principle of causality* should, were that principle true, be transferable to the *individual instances of causation,* to which the principle is applied. They will therefore argue: In the fact that one ball strikes another, where do you perceive a priori the intelligible necessity of the second ball's motion?

By simply inspecting the notions of which I have been speaking, to be contingent and to be caused, we see clearly that they are necessarily conjoined, and that the former demands the latter as that which accounts for its existence. But this does not mean that in every particular case we know in what this sufficient reason consists. I may remark, incidentally, that examples taken from psychology are preferable to others. Take the following example: I did this because I willed to do it, the instance of a rational and deliberate act of will. Here we see better how the effect, the act of choice, is attached to its cause, the deliberate will, as its sufficient reason. But even here a vast element of mystery remains, both in respect of the action of the cause, the free will itself, and of the fashion in which this decision is translated externally by a particular bodily movement.

3. Speaking generally it would seem that the mystery of being deepens when we come to the principle of causality. The reasons of this we may find in the facts that it is a principle primarily existential, that the bringing of anything into existence is always invested with a peculiar mystery, and that being is strictly the effect of the first cause. It is only inasmuch as second causes are themselves moved by God that they impart existence to their effect, are able to *make anything exist*. Therefore in the production of existence, the efficacious vocation to existence, there is something which exceeds what a second cause could effect by itself, if it were not premoved by the First Cause, and which in some way depends upon the mystery of the creative act. ،

If a being is contingent, there must, of necessity, be something outside it which accounts for its coming into existence. Its own ontological sufficiency, if I may so put it, must be separate from it and bestowed upon it by another. This is certain, but *how* are we to understand it? In the first place we must not entertain the illusion that we have understood it by means of images which confine the mind to the empirical order and delude it with a false clarity—an illusion which plays into the hands of the nominalists and the Kantians. If we remain within the intelligible order and respect its mystery, we shall find that it is possible to penetrate a little way into the intelligible mystery, by employing the keys forged by Aristotle, namely potency and act, and recognizing the dynamic nature of being, the ontological root of the tendency, inclination, and love on which I insisted so strongly in my last lecture.

The principle of causality—every contingent being

has a cause—may be expressed more philosophically in terms of potency and act. We shall affirm: That every being compounded of potency and act inasmuch as it is potential does not pass of itself to act, does not *reduce* itself to act. It passes to act by the operation of another being in act which causes the change. *Nihil reducit se de potentia in actum.*

It is now clear that no being can be a cause save insofar as it is in act and (if a created cause) is confronted by a corresponding potency, a receptive factor. Being an agent is itself an inclination to communicate a good, so that philosophers who fail to recognize this dynamic aspect of being, and conceive being as an order of geometrical fixtures taken in the state of abstraction in which they exist in our mind, and sterilized of every tendency and consubstantial love, must inevitably, with Malebranche, find causality a stumbling block.

It is clear that the communication of being and good implied by the relation of cause to effect is not the transmission of any imaginable entity, solid or liquid, passing from the former to the latter, but a community of actuation that is at once the final perfection of the transitive agent and that of the patient, both thus sharing in a single act and the agent's action being in the patient, *actio in passo.* (In the case of an immanent action virtually transitive, the action as such is wholly accomplished in the agent. But it evokes in the patient the actuality which perfects it and thereby renders the agent present in the patient, that is itself simply an ontological obedience to the action.)

It is clear that since every created cause is as a cause *more than the effect:* and at the same time as created, *less than itself and the effect together:* in order to act it must be itself perfected, and brought into action by another. Nothing therefore, absolutely nothing, could be produced here below, not the slightest stir of a leaf, not the tiniest ripple on the surface of water, not the lightest movement of the emotions, not the most insignificant act of thought or will, if the created universe were not *open* to the action, virtually transitive, of the pure *act,* which, as Aristotle said, touches it without being touched by it, if a continual current of causal efficacy were not being poured without ceasing into creatures from the bosom of subsistent Intellect and subsistent Love. This is what is termed, in barbarous phraseology, physical premotion.

Supplementary Remarks

4. The same observation must be made about the principle of causality as about the principles of sufficient reason and finality. It is a proposition intrinsically necessary, self-evident, but pertaining to the second mode of *perseity*. It is not in the notion which constitutes the subject that we perceive that of the attribute. The predicate is neither part of the definition of the subject nor the definition itself. It is the subject which is involved by the predicate as its *specific subject*. If we compare—for even when it intuits the first principles of reason the mind actively compares—these two notions, *contingent being* and *caused being, that is, being that has the ground of its existence in another,* we see that the specific subject of that which has the ground of its existence in another is precisely contingent being.

5. I should like to put before you some further observations on the principle of causality. The first concerns its application to living beings. How does it apply to them? The classical definition of life appears to contradict the principle of causality. For it defines a living being as a being that moves itself. But we have just said that nothing can reduce itself from potency to act, can cause itself.' The contradiction is merely apparent. Living beings certainly move themselves. But they do not move in the same respect as that in which they are moved. This is obvious in the case of material organisms. One part moves another. Certainly the organism does move itself. For

the two parts are not two distinct substances, but two parts of a single substance. Nevertheless, one part moves another.

In the case of an immaterial faculty such as the intelligence or the will, which has no parts, it is still untrue that it moves and is moved under the same aspect, in the same respect. The will, for example, reduces itself to act, moves itself in respect of the means inasmuch as it is already in act in respect of the end, that it wills that end in act, and it is because it wills the end in act that it is itself the cause of willing the means. Thus the principle of causality is always safeguarded.

We must further add that in the case of all these living beings whose self-motion involves a passage from potency to act and which move themselves because they are in act in one respect, in potency in another, we must admit the action of a First Cause, a Prime Agent who moves them to move themselves. Only the absolute life, life as it is found in God, realizes the notion of life so perfectly that it depends on no cause. All living beings other than God move themselves, only because they are moved by another. There is another, namely, the First Cause of all being, that moves them or determines them to move themselves, without thereby contradicting the notion of life or destroying their vital autonomy.

6. Another observation concerns the procession of immanent acts. How far can we speak of an efficient cause in their case? Consider, for example, an act of intelligence or will. Such acts, as I have already observed —and I am not speaking of their product, the mental word, for instance, but of the act of intelligence (or will) —are *qualities* which perfect the subject. We have already seen that the immanent act belongs to the predicament quality, and insofar as it thus signifies a perfection, it does not require, in virtue of its purest notion, to be caused. That is why such acts are realized in uncaused Being, the pure Act. But wherever the act differs from the acting subject—insofar as it is distinct from the faculty and the subject and therefore is *produced*—a sub-

ject in another respect in act determines himself from potency to act and "produces" something which is not an object, but an action, the act itself of understanding or willing. He does not produce it by some other act. The act is itself at once a quality and an emanation. To that extent then a process of this kind comes under the principle and notion of causality, the act has a sufficient reason other than itself, that is a cause, which is above all the activity, the active power of the subject himself.

Many other questions might be discussed concerning efficient casuality. The fact should be emphasized that the notion of cause, like that of being, is essentially analogous. We should thus reach the conclusion that God is cause, indeed pre-eminently cause, that it is as the cause of being that reason is compelled to recognize His existence, though His causality is not like that of any cause we know. All this, however, must be reserved for treatment elsewhere, as also the examination of certain problems raised by contemporary philosophers, for example by M. Brunschvicg, in his monograph on physical causality.[1] I shall be content here with the very summary hints I have just thrown out, which, however, will convey my meaning and which are strictly within the scope of my lectures. '

---

[1] I regret that it was impossible to deal, in the earlier chapters of this work, with the views of M. Louis Lavelle and his book, *La Dialectique de l'Eternel Présent: de l'Etre* (Alcan). But the discussion which this would have involved would have taken me outside the field of these lectures. I also regret that it was impossible to make use of A. Marc's important monograph: *L'Idée de l'Etre chez St. Thomas et dans la scolastique postérieure*, Archives de philosophie, volume X, cahier I, Beauchesne, 1933. The lectures were finished before it was published.

Chance

7. I must, however, speak about a problem bound up with that of causality, namely the problem of chance. Bear well in mind the philosophic and ontological character of the notion of efficient causation, such as I have attempted to elicit it. The efficient cause is an external ground which, to put it so, renders intelligible, I do not say to us, but in itself, the existence of an object or event. This conception of a cause carries with it another conception, that of the communication of being. And the efficient cause is an agent predetermined to a particular effect as the tree is predetermined to its fruit, living energy to local motion, hydrogen and oxygen to produce water under given conditions. We must keep before our minds this philosophic and ontological conception of the efficient cause if we are to obtain an accurate notion of chance. It is because the essentially ontological character of the conception of cause is too often forgotten that the Aristotelian and Thomist theory of chance is no longer correctly understood.

Chance, a fortuitous event, presupposes the mutual interference of independent lines of causation. Chance, and this is the basis of the ancients' notion of it, is the result of an irreducible pluralism, the plurality of the causal series which meet at a given moment. It is not the fact that it cannot be foreseen that constitutes chance. A fortuitous event can be foreseen, if its constituent factors are sufficiently simple. But it is a fortuitous event notwithstanding, since it is a mere *encounter*.

You may remember Aristotle's example. Is it true to say that a man is killed by brigands *because* he has eaten too salt viands? What is the link here between cause and effect? He has eaten too salt viands, becomes thirsty, and goes out to a spring. Behind the spring brigands are in hiding who profit by the opportunity to murder him. There is a chain of causes and effects. Is the entire chain necessary? To understand the conception of chance, which is far more difficult than is often supposed, we shall examine this instance of it. There are here three series of causes. One extends from the salt food to the thirst. It is normal and in the natural order of things that salt food should cause thirst, the thirst excite the desire to drink, and the desire lead to the action. In another series there is a preliminary condition that there should be no water in the house. Moreover, there must be a spring near. And its existence in the vicinity must itself have a cause, namely the presence in a particular locality of underground water which in turn depends upon an entire series of geological facts. There is a third series of causes which accounts for the presence of the brigands at that particular place. Their presence there depends, for example, on their having hidden in the woods from the pursuit of the police, and this is itself the result of previous crimes they have committed. Thus three independent casual chains meet, and the man's death is the result of their meeting. Each of the causes here operative continues or would have continued to act in its own line. The brigands would have continued their career of robbery, the spring its casual action, erosion of the earth's surface, evaporation, etc., and had the victim not met his death, the drink he had taken would have produced a particular physiological effect upon his organism. Every event in each series of causes has therefore its cause within the series. But the encounter between an event of one series, for example, the presence of the brigands and events of the other two, the existence of the spring and the desire to drink has not as such any cause in the entire universe. That is to say there is no nature, no natural agent predetermined by its structure to this encounter of the three events, nor any created intelligence that designed it.

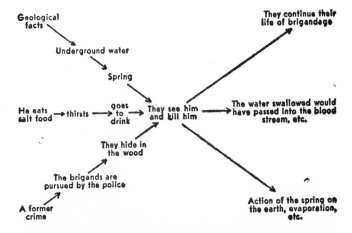

The illustrative diagram makes clear the irreducible multiplicity in which chance consists. Each of three casual lines diverges from the rest as we trace the series backward, so that the farther back we go in each series, the more remote are we from the possibility of finding a cause predetermined to the meeting of the three series and accounting for it. ·

That is to say the encounter of the three casual lines at a given moment is indeed a *contingent* fact but not a contingent *being.* This is the difficult and important point to grasp in the theory of chance. The encounter has no *being,* save in thought. Certainly it exists. But it is not an essence. It is a pure coincidence, and possesses no ontological unity requiring to render its existence intelligible an active structure preordained to it. It is neither a genuine being nor a genuine unity, and therefore does not possess a genuine cause, in the ontological sense which I have explained.

8. You will find these notions explained by St. Thomas in what is, in my opinion, his deepest treatment of the Fortuitous, in the Prima Pars of his *Summa* 115, 6. He is inquiring whether the heavenly bodies necessitate all events. In reality he treats here in another language the

entire problem of mechanism. His answer might seem at first sight paradoxical. "Arguing," he says, "from the propositions that everything has a cause and on the other hand that when the cause is present the effect necessarily follows (are not these two propositions evident?) some have drawn the conclusion that all things happen of necessity. Their opinion is refuted by Aristotle in the sixth book of the *Metaphysics*. And his refutation deals precisely with the two propositions to which these men appeal. In the first place, he says, it is not true that if any cause whatever is present the effect necessarily follows. For there are some causes which do not produce their effects necessarily, but only in the majority of cases, and such causes sometimes fail to produce the effect only in a very small number of instances." (It suffices that the cause predetermined of itself to a particular effect, for example a medicine preordained to heal the organism, is prevented from producing *its* effect.)

"But," St. Thomas proceeds, "since these causes fail in a particular instance only because another cause intervenes to prevent their normal effect, would it not seem that our opponents are after all right? For this hindrance itself has a cause and therefore happens of necessity. It must, therefore, be said in the second place that everything which is of itself, *omne quod est per se,* everything that constitutes an essence in the strict sense, is in the strict sense a being, has a cause. That, however, which is by accident, has no cause, *quia non est vere ens cum non sit vere unum,* for it is not genuine being, because it is not truly one."

It is important to remember this last statement. Since for lack of ontological unity there is no genuine being, there is, therefore, no need of a cause of which the event in question is the effect, a cause in the nature of which the effect is predetermined. "But it is clear that when one cause prevents the action of another, the preventing cause interferes with the former *per accidens,* accidentally. Wherefore, such an encounter of causes has no cause, inasmuch as it happens accidentally. Therefore what follows upon such an encounter cannot be reduced to a particular pre-existent cause from which it follows of necessity. Thus, when a fiery meteor is formed in a particular region of the air, the cause of the event is to be found in the power of the heavenly bodies." (The cause which determines it is the constitution of the universe, whose essential structure requires this effect.) '

"Similarly that on a particular spot on the earth's surface there should be certain combustible materials can also be reduced to causes dependent upon the heavenly bodies. But that the fire when it falls should encounter those materials and burn them, and the two series of causes should thus intersect, is not caused by any heavenly body." (That is to say, there is no agent, no essential structure which of its nature requires it.) *"Non habet causam aliquod coeleste corpus, sed est per accidens.* It is not caused by any heavenly body, but happens accidentally."

Chance is thus reduced to the plurality of which I was speaking just now. Consult also St. Thomas's last lecture, Lecture 14, on the first book of the Perihermeneias. In each of the independent causal series there studied there is a chain of causes and effects. But the encounter between them does not depend upon any cause determined by its nature to produce it and requiring its occurrence. The fire caused by the thunderbolt is an event which replaces that which would naturally have followed in the causal series. Take, for example, the accumulation of dried vegetable matter in the soil of a particular place. The next event in the same causal chain might have been that these dried vegetables would have helped to manure the ground. The series would thus have continued in the same line. This event, however, to which of itself the preceding event would have led did not take place. For the series was interrupted by its encounter with another series of causes belonging to the meteorological order.

9. To obtain a complete idea of the theory we must add St. Thomas's explanations in the following article (q. 116, a. I). He there points out that that which is accidental may be unified by a mind. In that case the en-

counter, the intersection of causes which constitutes chance and does not constitute a being with a unity of its own outside the mind, but is the pure coincidence of many factors, possesses a unity in the mind that knows it, and above all in the Mind that is the cause of nature. And this encounter as it is known by that Mind can also be caused by It, can depend upon Its providence which disposes all things and has disposed this entire manifold, this infinite multitude of individual causes and their interferences.

From this it is evident that we must improve our statement of the principle of causality. Everything we said which exists or happens contingently or mingled with potency has a cause. Now we must add: in accordance with the requirements of its being or unity. If what exists or happens contingently is not *vere ens,* genuine being, not *ens per se,* being by itself, but *ens per accidens,* accidental being, possesses only a conceptual being and unity as the mutual interference of a manifold, its sole *cause* can be a thought on which the causal series which thus meet depend. That is to say, in the case of fortuitous events conditioned neither by a human nor by an angelic intelligence, their cause, the cause which aims at such an effect can be only the Mind, the Intelligence that knows all things. This fact invests fortuitous events with a peculiar interest. For they clearly depend, if we may so put it, more immediately, in respect of their predetermination, upon the First Cause, than do other events.

On the other hand we understand what the ancients meant when they called chance an accidental cause, *causa per accidens,* or *natura agens praeter intentionem,* a natural agent acting outside its determination to an end. Why does it so act? Because it has encountered another causal series. See further on this topic the important explanations by Aristotle and St. Thomas.[2]

All this amounts to saying that the simple intersection of different causal chains is not in itself more intelligible

---

[2] Book II of the *Physics* with St. Thomas's lectures 7 to 10, and Book XI of the *Metaphysics* with St. Thomas's lecture, and Book XII with his third lecture.

than the event which results from it. The explanation of the fortuitous fact or event must be sought in the causes active in each of these causal chains. But none of these causes is predetermined to produce it, and this multiplicity of causes explains the chance event only on the supposition that these chains meet at a particular point of intersection. And there is nothing in the world which requires this, save the actual manifold of existents posited at the outset. There is no agent whose nature is such that it must overflow in this particular effect and is fore-ordained to produce it. We say: "This chance event occurs *because* a particular event has occurred before it, *because* these two causal series have crossed." That is to say, we unite this manifold in our mind. But there is no being whose structure and essential preordination postulate of themselves this encounter.

· It is equally clear that chance cannot possibly be the origin of things. For it presupposes an encounter of causal series, and further that each of these series exists only because the causes it contains are determined to a particular end. Chance, that is to say, necessarily implies preordination. To hold that the universe can be explained by a primordial chance is self-contradictory.

10. This theory of chance is as philosophical, as ontological in its character and statement, employs notions as strictly metaphysical as the preceding theory of causation. If your conception of cause is purely empirical or empiriological, if you empty it of all philosophic or ontological content and with the empiricists make it consist solely in the observed fact of a constant precedence, you will be unable to distinguish between what is necessary and what is fortuitous. It is thus only what we should have expected, that as positive science has replaced cause by a purely empirical substitute, it has tended in the same measure to adopt a statistical theory of causation, a statistical determinism, of recent years statistical indeterminism intended to replace genuine causal determinism. We may further observe, and still with the same considerations in view, that a difficulty

may be raised about the application of the principle of finality to ordered manifold. Take the case not of an agent predetermined to its distinctive effect, but of a united plurality, a manifold united like that of an orchestra, in short, a case of *order*. For order is essentially a manifold reduced to unity. It is usually said, and with perfect truth, it is indeed an expression of finality, that order presupposes someone who produces it having himself the intention to impose this unity on the manifold. And there is a fundamental reason for affirming this to which St. Thomas frequently appeals: A manifold cannot possibly by itself account for its unity. *Multa per se intendunt ad multa, unus vero ad unum.*

If this be granted, we may ask whether the principle is universally applicable. Are there not instances in which we believe that a manifold has been intentionally ordered when in reality this is not the case? Can we not see shapes in the clouds or on old walls, such as Leonardo da Vinci liked to trace? Can we not form a word by chance when we combine the letters of the alphabet at random? They may be selected at random and nevertheless form an intelligible word, at any rate a very short one. We may then imagine that the word has been intentionally formed and written. What answer shall we return to this difficulty, which is a serious one? For by applying mathematics to any particular instance of order we may inquire what is the probability of its chance realization. What, for example, is the mathematical probability that by combining all the letters of the alphabet an enormous number of times a poem such as the *Iliad* might be composed? The mathematician will ask this question. He will answer it by calculating the improbability, which will indeed be enormous. But his calculation itself implies that however enormous the improbability, it is not an impossibility.

To answer this problem we must, I believe, maintain that if a unity is genuine, and consequently the order in question is real, our principle admits no exception. The order depends on one who has ordered it, a cause of unity whose intelligence has in view the unity of this manifold. Therefore everything depends on the question whether the unity is real or merely apparent. For since, as St. Thomas pointed out, what is not of itself one may be united in the mind, there may be a conceptual or apparent without a real unity. The entire problem, therefore, reduces itself to this: To find a criterion whereby we can distinguish a real unity existing outside the mind from a purely conceptual unity. The mathematician leaves this problem out of account. For him the distinction between real and conceptual existence has no interest. He will therefore submit to the calculus of probabilities, things, cases, problems which *in reality* are not amenable to this treatment. If, for example, a poem possesses a real unity, not merely the semblance of unity, really expresses an intelligible organism—I am not speaking of surrealist poems, though even in their case random thinking presupposes thought—if the universe in the same way possesses a real unity verifiable by the constancy of particular actions and laws which subserve the conservation of the whole, it is metaphysically *impossible,* not merely improbable but impossible, that this order should be produced without someone to produce it. The mathematician, however, remains free to make his calculation of probabilities, because as such he does not inquire whether he is working with real or conceptual beings.

III

11. In these lectures I have dealt only with the first four principles of speculative reason. But they are very far from exhausting the number of self-evident principles. A fifth concerns formal causation. It may be stated as follows: "Everything which exists is formed and determined," or in other terms, "Every determination is a perfection insofar as it is due to form, a limitation insofar as it depends upon matter." A sixth concerns material

causation. It runs: "Every change presupposes a subject."
A seventh declares: *"Operatio sequitur esse.* Operation
follows being."

There are also principles which are corollaries of these
great primary axioms. For example the principle of sufficient reason, and the principle of causality, involve the
four following subordinate principles. *Propter quod
unumquodque et illud magis, aut saltem non minus*—that
in virtue of which anything is must be greater or at least
not less than it. *Id propter quod aliquid est, oportet
melius esse*—that in virtue of which anything is must be
better than it. *Quod est per se (per suam essentiam)
prius est eo quod non est per se*—that which is by itself
(by its essence) is prior to that which is not by itself.
*Omne quod habet aliquid per participationem reducitur
ad id quod habet illud per essentiam sicut in principium
et causam*—whatsoever possesses anything by participation is reducible to that which possesses it by its essence
as its principle and cause.[3]

You will find in St. Thomas's *Compendium Theologiae*
a veritable treasury of such metaphysical axioms. It
would be of great interest to draw up a methodical list
of them.

And we should do well to build up metaphysical
axiomatics in the same spirit.

[3] See on these points my *Antimoderne*, pp. 179 sqq.